THE
IRISH-AMERICAN
ANSWER BOOK

The Ethnic Answer Books

The African-American Answer Book
The German-American Answer Book
The Irish-American Answer Book
The Jewish-American Answer Book

The Ethnic Answer Books

THE IRISH-AMERICAN ANSWER BOOK

Ellen Shnidman

General Editors
Sandra Stotsky
Harvard Graduate School of Education

Reed Ueda
Tufts University

Chelsea House Publishers • Philadelphia

CHELSEA HOUSE PUBLISHERS

Editor in Chief: Stephen Reginald
Managing Editor: James D. Gallagher
Production Manager: Pamela Loos
Art Director: Sara Davis
Picture Editor: Judy L. Hasday
Senior Production Editor: Lisa Chippendale
Associate Art Director/Designer: Takeshi Takahashi

First Printing

1 3 5 7 9 8 6 4 2

Library of Congress Cataloging-in-Publication Data

Shnidman, Ellen.
The Irish-American answer book / Ellen Shnidman : general editors, Sandra Stotsky, Reed Ueda.
  p. cm. — (The ethnic answer books)
Includes bibliographical references (p.) and index.
Summary: Presents questions covering the history, culture and social life, religion, political activities, economic life, and accomplishments of Irish Americans, with a separate section of answers.

ISBN 0-7910-4795-4 (hc.)
ISBN 0-7910-4796-2 (pbk.)

1. Irish Americans—Miscellanea—Juvenile literature. 2. Questions and answers—Juvenile literature. [1. Irish Americans—Miscellanea. 2. Questions and answers.] I. Stotsky, Sandra. II. Ueda, Reed. III. Title. IV. Series: Shnidman, Ellen. Ethnic answer books.
E184.I6S56 1998
973'.049162—dc21   98-16219
                                                          CIP
                                                          AC

CONTENTS

278/912-A

Introduction
ETHNIC ANSWER BOOKS

O ver half a century ago, Louis Adamic, a Slovenian immigrant who had become a popular writer, described the United States as a country "all of a piece, a blend of cultures from many lands, woven of threads from many corners of the world." The history of the United States shows that this nation has indeed been woven from many strands. More immigrants and more ethnic groups have come to live in America than in any other country in the world. In fact, the United States has been the most powerful magnet for international migration in world history.

Extensive immigration began in the 17th century when English settlers began to colonize North America, intermingling with the early Dutch settlers as well as the indigenous peoples of this continent. Blacks also came in large numbers, imported from Africa to serve as slaves. Well before the American Revolution, other groups of people—the Germans, French Huguenots, Scots, Welsh, and Scotch-Irish were the major groups—also began to migrate here. After the American Revolution, the United States' favorable immigration policies led to a large influx of immigrants, who helped settle and develop the new country. From 1820 to 1930, 38,000,000 people moved to the United States while 24,000,000 people migrated to Canada, Argentina, Brazil, Australia, New Zealand, South Africa, and other areas. From World War II to the early 1990s, 20,000,000 newcomers flocked to the United States. As a result of these continuous waves of migration to America's shores, the United States and Canada have evolved into multi-ethnic countries of remarkable proportions, with each having absorbed an enormous variety of ethnic groups.

Educators at all levels are now encouraging greater attention to the many dimensions of American diversity, especially our religious and ethnic diversity. As a part of their study of American history, students are now being asked to learn about the Irish, Italians, Chinese, Poles, Mexicans, and Germans—to name some of our country's major immigrant ethnic groups—as well as the African Americans and the indigenous peoples of this continent. Indeed, the distinctive characteristics and contributions of all this country's ethnic groups have now taken a place at the center of our school curriculum.

This new series of educational texts seeks to provide secondary students with a handy and compact reference work they can use to learn how a democratic nation was built out of intermixture and interdependence. All the volumes in this series are similar in three important respects. Every volume has a question and answer format. Each book supplies a core of factual information about a particular ethnic group. And all the volumes are organized by common chapters.

The creators of this series have designed this format to accomplish several educational goals. First, we offer questions about key features of the group's life and history in order to arouse students' curiosity about this particular group of Americans. Questions also serve to provide models of inquiry for students; these are the kinds of questions a historian asks when seeking to understand the history and life of a group of people. Second, the answers we provide to these questions are designed to yield a nucleus of significant facts. These facts can be drawn on for research reports, and they can serve as a point of departure for further inquiry into the history and experiences of an ethnic group. Finally, all the questions are organized into common chapters across all books in the series so that students can make informative comparisons and contrasts among American ethnic groups.

The first two chapters in each volume deal with the group's origins and arrival in America. The next three chapters provide information on the group's economic, religious, and social life and institutions in this country. Another three chapters present information on the group's distinctive characteristics, intellectual and cultural life, and participation in American public life. The final chapter describes important or accomplished individuals in this group's history in America. By comparing and contrasting information in these chapters among various ethnic groups, students have an excellent opportunity to learn about many significant features of American life, both in the past and today. They can learn about the different ways that each group has drawn on America's political principles and institutions to integrate its members into American political life. They can discover the different ways that America's ethnic groups interacted with each other as well as with the descendants of the English settlers who framed this country's political principles and institutions. They can find out how members of each group took advantage of this country's free public schools and free public libraries to advance themselves socially, intellectually, and economically. And students can begin to understand the remarkable similarities in the experiences of many ethnic groups in this country despite their having come from many different parts of the world, as well as the remarkable differences among ethnic groups who have come from the same parts of the world.

It is our hope that this series of books will serve as an intellectual guidepost to further student learning. It will help supply a solid foundation of knowledge that students can draw on to supplement what they learn in their classes on American history, literature, and government. And students will learn how to ask "good" questions about ethnicity. They will learn from the answers that it is a subject full of surprises and complexity—that ethnicity is not equivalent to race or language, that an ethnic group's characteristics depend heavily on when large numbers of its members arrive in this country, and that a group's characteristics change markedly from generation to generation in America. As a result, students will find the study of ethnic history a fascinating experience of discovery about how this country became the most successful democracy in history.

—Sandra Stotsky and Reed Ueda

Foreword
THE IRISH AMERICANS

F rom the first English settlements at Plymouth and Jamestown until at least two centuries later, the society that became the United States of America was predominantly Protestant. The mass immigration of Irish Catholics to America beginning in the early 19th century started a transformation of American society that continues today. The Irish were one of the first immigrant groups that helped mold America into a pluralistic society where people may be culturally different but remain politically equal, coexisting peacefully. The Irish experience in America also transformed one of the most downtrodden, oppressed, and impoverished groups of people in the world into an American success story.

The first Irish immigrants arrived in America in the 17th and 18th centuries. Most of these were Scotch Irish—that is, Protestants from the northern part of Ireland. They settled in the mid-Atlantic and southeastern part of the country in rural areas. Fairly quickly, most of them merged with the dominant Anglo-Protestant population of that region. Those who remained distinct lived mostly in the isolated hamlets of Appalachia well into the 20th century.

The bulk of the Irish immigrant population that came to America arrived in the 19th century. These Irish immigrants were mostly Catholics from the south and west of Ireland. They were fleeing grinding poverty, overpopulation, and British domination. The largest single wave of Irish immigrants arrived between 1845 and 1855. These were famine refugees—people fleeing the severe crop failures that led to starvation and death.

The Irish arrived in the United States from the small towns of rural Ireland with little education and no experience with urban life. They crowded into slums in the eastern cities or shanty towns along the railroads and canals of America, which they helped to build. From the appalling conditions of the "wild Irish slums," where mortality from disease, malnutrition, and alcoholism was as bad as it was in Ireland, the Irish-Catholic immigrants began their upward journey in America.

Irish Catholics were largely responsible for creating and shaping the character of three important American institutions: the urban political machines, the labor unions, and the Catholic Church. These institutions have played an enduring role in American society. When the Irish arrived in America, they settled mostly in the big cities of the East and Midwest. Anglo-Protestants held the power in these cities and, because of cultural and religious differences, did not care for the Irish. The Anglo-Protestants largely monopolized the business world and professional life of American society into the 20th century, so Irish immigrants turned to political and religious institutions as ways to improve their economic status.

By the 1870s Irish Catholics were the largest ethnic group in most large American cities. Quin O'Brien, an Irish-American politician of the early 20th century, remarked, "Politics favors the mixer and the spender." The Irish, with their characteristic comradery and charm and their networks of patronage, were well suited to build the great urban political machines of the late 19th and early 20th centuries. Getting a political appointment from city hall was the ticket out of the slums for many enterprising Irishmen.

The Catholic Church offered another path to respect and success. Irish Americans, from the earliest years of their immigration, began to build and manage the churches, schools, universities, and charitable institutions that are now run by Catholic archdioceses around the country. The Catholic school system has educated generations of Catholic Americans. Today it serves as an indispensable alternative to urban public schools for many poor African American and Hispanic families. Because of their population growth and because of the way they managed the Catholic Church, the Irish made Catholicism a major religious denomination in America. The acceptance of Roman Catholicism was a major step toward guaranteeing that America would remain a pluralistic society open to many denominations and religious faiths.

Over the last two centuries the Irish strove to be accepted by the Anglo-Protestant majority and to achieve economic status. They have succeeded on both counts. These accomplishments would surprise those observers who initially predicted that Irish Catholics were an alien group of people who would never be accepted into the general population. The Irish have succeeded so well that very little survives of the distinct Irish neighborhoods and social life that once was such a large part of American urban life.

During the last 30 years, the nature of the Irish-American population has changed considerably. Many Irish have moved to the suburbs and become less intense in their religious devotion. The two institutions with which they were most associated—the Democratic Party and the Catholic Church—have suffered setbacks. The urban base of the Democratic Party has eroded, and many American cities now have Republican mayors. The Irish in suburbia increasingly vote for Republicans and do not play as large a role in political life as they once did. The Catholic Church has experienced a loss of priests and nuns to serve in its American institutions, and the number of Irish Americans choosing religious vocations has gone down dramatically, as has their leadership role in the laity.

On the other side of the ledger, many qualities that once were closely associated with the Irish have been absorbed into the broader American society. The personal quality of urban and national politics, parochial school education, the American fighting spirit on the battlefield and on athletic playing fields, and the open congeniality of the American personality are all characteristics that owe much of their origins to the waves of Irish immigrants who came to America for a better life.

—Ellen Shnidman

Questions

◀ The Celtic Cross is one of the most popular memorial crosses. The crosses started to appear in Ireland in the fourth and fifth centuries, after the island was invaded by Danes. The cross design is influenced by Byzantine architecture because of Denmark's trade with the nations of the East where the Byzantine Catholic Church flourished. The crosses also served an educational purpose, as the stories of the Christian religion were often carved onto the stone, as in this example.

ORIGINS

Ireland Under English Rule

1-1   What group of people were the first to invade Ireland?

1-2   From where did the Celtic tribes come?

1-3   What group of people invaded Ireland in the late 8th century A.D. and introduced significant changes in its society?

1-4   When did the British arrive in Ireland and in what way?

1-5   Originally both England and Ireland were Catholic countries. What event changed this situation?

1-6   How did the establishment of the Anglican Church affect relations between the English and the Irish?

1-7   Why did English monarchs encourage the settlement of English and Scottish Protestants in the north of Ireland during the 17th century?

1-8   By what name did the Scottish Protestants who settled in the north of Ireland become known in America?

1-9 How did the Irish Protestants and Catholics from the north of Ireland differ at the time of immigration to America in the 18th and 19th centuries, as well as today?

1-10 What have relations been like between Protestants and Catholics in Ireland over the centuries?

1-11 In the early 19th century, Ireland was one of the poorest places in Europe. A French visitor compared the condition of Irish peasants to that of black slaves in America. Why did he think the Irish lived under more miserable conditions?

1-12 What was one of the reasons for Ireland's poverty in the 18th and 19th centuries?

1-13 By the 1800s Ireland's agricultural economy was largely based on one crop. What crop was this?

1-14 Why did Irish peasants prefer to cultivate this crop?

1-15 What is the danger in having an agricultural economy based only on one crop?

1-16 What was the original language of Ireland?

1-17 How did Ireland go from being a Gaelic-speaking country in the 17th century to an overwhelmingly English-speaking country in the 20th century?

1-18 Have there been attempts to revive the Gaelic language in Ireland?

1-19 What political act by the British government in 1801 tied the fate of Ireland to Great Britain?

1-20 What were the Penal Laws that were enacted by the English rulers of Ireland? What was their intended purpose?

1-21 In 1829 Daniel O'Connell's movement for Catholic emancipation achieved success. What did his movement accomplish?

1-22 After Catholics got the vote in 1829, O'Connell started another nonviolent political movement. What was the purpose of his second movement?

The Creation of Two Irelands

1-23 In what year was Sinn Fein, the Irish nationalist movement, founded?

1-24 What does *sinn fein* mean in the Gaelic language?

1-25 The British Liberal Party came to power in 1912 and supported home rule for the Irish. What was the reaction of the Ulster Protestants?

1-26 Irish home rule was declared by the British Parliament in 1914, but the implementation of this law was delayed. What was the cause of the delay?

1-27 At Easter time in 1916, an uprising took place in Dublin called the Easter Rising or Rebellion. What was the purpose of this uprising?

1-28 What happened to the Irish Republican Brotherhood leaders of this uprising who were not killed during the military action itself?

1-29 In 1918, the general elections in Ireland produced a massive victory for Sinn Fein. What action did Sinn Fein take?

1-30 After several years of civil war, Ireland was partitioned by the Anglo-Irish Treaty of 1921. How was the island partitioned?

1-31 In 1949 Ireland was proclaimed a republic. How did this change the political status of the country?

1-32 What was the status of Northern Ireland until 1972?

Contemporary Ireland

1-33 What is the current relationship between Irish Protestants and Catholics in Northern Ireland?

1-34 How is the conflict between the Protestants and Catholics expressed?

1-35 Is the conflict in Northern Ireland likely to be resolved soon?

1-36 Today the Republic of Ireland is undergoing an economic renaissance. What has brought about this revival?

1-37 There is also a cultural revival going on in Ireland, particularly in the arts and letters. What is one sign of this?

1-38 What change in population movement has occurred in the last few years that is a new phenomenon for Ireland?

1-39 How have the improved economic circumstances in the Irish Republic influenced Sinn Fein and nationalist Catholic opinion in Northern Ireland?

1-40 What are relations like today between the Irish Republic and Great Britain?

Irish Saints

rish Catholics believe their saints can do extraordinary things. Some well-known Irish saints and their exploits:

St. Brendan (484–578) was also known as "Brendan the Navigator" for his skills on the sea. Many believe he may have discovered North America on one of his voyages between the years A.D. 535 and 553.

St. Brigid (460–528) was a nun who dedicated her life to missionary work and founded a famous religious house in Kildare. When she was a child, St. Brigid and her mother were sold to a wizard by her father, a pagan king. Her generosity to the poor is the source of many miraculous legends.

St. Colmcille (521–597) set up a chain of monasteries. He was known for promoting many Irish traditions in the Catholic church. Monks from his monastery at Iona spread Christianity through much of Scotland and northern England.

By far the greatest Irish saint, however, was St. Patrick, a missionary and bishop who helped spread Christianity throughout Ireland around the year 400. When he was 16, he was captured and sold into slavery in Ireland. Years later, he escaped by walking over 200 miles to freedom. Tradition holds that St. Patrick drove all the snakes out of Ireland.

St. Patrick's Day is the most widely celebrated Irish holiday in America, as the festivities in major American cities can attest. One of the more bizzare March 17 events occurs at the University of Missouri. Festivities open there with the "Snake Invasion," where rubber snakes are placed all over campus for students to "kill" with festive whacking sticks. But parades seem to be the most common form of celebration in America on March 17. Chicago prepares for its St. Patrick's Day parade by dyeing the city's river green for the week. Savannah, Georgia, claims its parade is the longest and largest in America, with over 200 floats traveling 3.2 miles. Boston's parade is also over 3 miles long. But it would be hard to beat New York's St. Patrick's Day parade. Founded in 1762, it is the oldest celebration of its kind in the country. The New York St. Patrick's Day parade has recently averaged 150,000 marchers, 2 to 3 million observers, and an astounding 5 1/2 hours.

◀ Hell's Kitchen was a notorious New York City slum where thousands of Irish immigrants lived. The Irish were the first ethnic group to settle predominantly in the cities, particularly in New York, Philadelphia, and Boston.

CHAPTER

2

ARRIVAL IN AMERICA

Waves of Immigration

2-1 When did the Irish to begin to immigrate to America?

2-2 What was the religious background of most of the immigrants to America from Ireland in the 1700s?

2-3 What was one of the main motivations for Ulster Presbyterians (Scotch Irish) to leave Ireland and emigrate to America in the 18th century?

2-4 In what century did the huge waves of Irish-Catholic immigration to the United States and Canada begin?

2-5 About one-third of the Irish immigration to the United States in the 19th century occurred during a five-year period. When was this period? What caused this massive emigration from Ireland?

2-6 The Irish who immigrated to America continued to speak English. How did this affect their ability to maintain relationships with family members still in Ireland? Why was this important?

2-7   In what region of the United States did the Scotch Irish settle?

2-8   Many Scotch-Irish immigrants settled along the Appalachian Mountain ridge in the 18th and 19th centuries. What was the attraction of such a remote, isolated, and underdeveloped region of the country?

2-9   The Scotch Irish, unlike the Irish Catholics, chose to settle in mountainous areas like Appalachia or the Ozarks or in small towns. For what lifestyle did some of them become known?

2-10   What colony was the only one of the original thirteen that provided freedom of worship for Catholics and thus attracted many of the earliest Irish-Catholic immigrants during the colonial period?

2-11   Where was America's first Roman Catholic Cathedral built? Who laid the cornerstone for the building?

2-12   What settlement patterns made Irish Catholics different from earlier European groups that had come to this country?

2-13   Why did so few Irish-Catholic immigrants become farmers when they arrived in America?

2-14   In the mid to late 1800s, New York City was the largest and most important American commercial and cultural center. Although Anglo-Protestants were the dominant group both socially and economically, what two ethnic groups had the largest populations?

2-15   By the 20th century, in New York City the Irish and Germans were surpassed in numbers by two other ethnic groups. What two groups were these?

2-16 By the late 19th century, major cities of America were known for neighborhoods made up of certain ethnic groups. What were the names of some of the urban neighborhoods associated with the Irish-American population?

2-17 How many of these neighborhoods are predominantly Irish today?

2-18 What happened to the descendants of the original residents of these neighborhoods?

2-19 Did the third- and fourth-generation Irish reestablish ethnic communities in the suburbs?

2-20 What region of the United States has the highest concentration of people who claim Irish ancestry?

◀ John Cardinal O'Connor, Archbishop of New York, waves to crowds during a 1993 St. Patrick's Day celebration. The Irish were the first large Catholic ethnic group in the United States, and Irish Americans continue to hold many important church leadership positions.

RELIGIOUS LIFE

Irish Protestants and Catholics

3-1   In what century did Ireland become Christian?

3-2   What has been the religious composition of Ireland since the early 18th century, when massive emigration to America began, until today?

3-3   The Scotch-Irish immigrants to America established one of America's most important denominations of Protestantism. What church was this?

3-4   The Presbyterian Church in America later divided into different branches. What was one of the main causes of factionalism in this church?

The Catholic Church in Ireland

3-5   Historically, what position has Catholicism had in Ireland?

3-6   What role has Ireland traditionally played in the world of European Catholicism?

3-7   What cultural function did the Catholic Church play in Ireland that was unusual for a Catholic country in Europe?

3-8   During the years that led up to the Catholic Emancipation (1829) and during the long campaign for home rule that followed, why did Catholicism play such a central role in Irish political life?

Catholic Life in America

3-9   How has the central role of Catholicism in Ireland expressed itself in the Irish contribution to American society?

3-10   How did the Irish mold and shape the Catholic Church in America?

3-11   How large a part of American church leadership were the Irish during the 20th century?

3-12   In the late 1800s German, Italian, and Polish Catholics resented the Irish domination of Catholic leadership. How did the Irish clergy respond to this discontent?

3-13   How did the Catholic Church in America during the 19th century view Irish nationalism?

3-14   Before the reforms of the 1960s, in what language was the Catholic mass celebrated?

3-15   What dietary restrictions were placed on meals eaten on Fridays in traditional Catholic homes years ago?

3-16   What Catholic bishop was a popular figure on national radio and television in the 1940s and '50s?

3-17 A number of big-city cardinals have become dominant figures in the cultural and political life of 20th-century American cities. Can you name a cardinal from Boston, New York, Philadelphia, or Chicago that has become nationally known in the last 40 years?

3-18 By the late 1970s, did Irish Americans still dominate the leadership of the Catholic Church as they did in the previous 100 years?

3-19 What changes were made in Catholicism by the Vatican II reforms of 1965?

3-20 The liberalizing reforms in the Catholic Church since the 1960s were supposed to increase the appeal of Catholicism to an increasingly educated lay population. Has this happened?

3-21 Why has there been a decline in the involvement of Irish Americans in the Catholic Church in recent generations?

3-22 The number of priests and nuns has declined in the last 30 years. This has hurt the Catholic school system and many individual parishes. What seems to be the main cause of this decline?

3-23 What other economic and social factors are responsible for the decline in the number of Irish Americans pursuing vocations in the church?

3-24 Irish success at fitting into the mainstream of American society is best symbolized by the celebration and prominence of what holiday in March?

3-25 How does the celebration of St. Patrick's Day in America differ from its celebration in Ireland?

CHAPTER

4

SOCIAL LIFE AND INSTITUTIONS

Ethnic Neighborhoods and Organizations

4-1 The single most important institution for Irish-Catholic immigrants and their children was the local parish. What role did the parish play?

4-2 What was the second most important institution for Irish immigrants and their children?

4-3 By the late 19th century Irish neighborhoods and shanty towns were widespread across America. What institutions were characteristic of Irish neighborhoods?

4-4 What was the most popular gathering place in an Irish neighborhood?

4-5 What social role did this gathering place play, especially for first- and second-generation Irish immigrants?

4-6 As in most urban neighborhoods of the period, the condition of Irish urban neighborhoods in mid-19th-century America was often appalling. What health problems did they frequently face?

4-7 By the late 19th century, Irish immigrants had created a variety of ethnic and civic organizations. Name some of these.

4-8 What was the other cultural force that characterized community life for first- and second-generation Irish immigrants?

4-9 What two popular Irish nationalist organizations were founded in America in the mid-1800s?

4-10 What did the Fenians hope to accomplish?

4-11 What caused the Fenians to split into two groups?

4-12 Were the Fenians successful?

4-13 What happened as a result of the Fenians' efforts?

4-14 In northern cities, relations between Irish immigrants and African Americans were often strained and marked by violence. What factors contributed to this problem?

The Catholic School System

4-15 In cities, the Catholic Church served as the glue that held together Irish-American communities for three generations. How did it serve this purpose?

4-16 The Catholic parochial school system in America was established and largely administered by Irish Catholics for generations. Why was the establishment of this school system an extraordinary accomplishment?

4-17 What was the original purpose for establishing the Catholic school system in the 19th century?

4-18 The Catholic school system reached its peak enrollment in the late 1950s and early 1960s. What percentage of Catholic children attended parochial school during that period?

4-19 What unique feature allowed the Catholic schools and colleges that were built in America over one hundred years ago to survive?

4-20 Why did enrollments in Catholic schools begin to fall in the 1960s until the early 1990s?

4-21 During the 1990s, Catholic schools in many regions of the country began to grow again. What is the reason for this?

4-22 How has the role of the inner-city Catholic school changed over the years? What vital role does it have today?

4-23 There are about 200 Catholic colleges and universities in America. Can you name at least one of the Catholic universities established by Irish Catholics?

The Scotch Irish

4-24 In the late 1800s and early 1900s, families of the Appalachian Mountains became known for what type of conflict?

4-25 What famous clan feud erupted in 1863, lasted for 30 years, and later became a symbol of this region in popular culture?

4-26 What happened to the majority of the descendants of the Scotch-Irish immigrants who did not settle in mountainous areas?

◀ For centuries, bagpipes have been identified with the Celtic races that inhabited Ireland. The bagpipe was introduced to England by conquering Romans nearly 2,000 years ago, and use of the instrument quickly spread to Ireland, where it became integrated into Celtic military and social life. This young bagpiper is one of a group of musicians marching in New York City's 1995 St. Patrick's Day parade.

CHAPTER

5

GROUP CHARACTERISTICS

Numbers and Descriptions

5-1 How many immigrants have come to the United States from Ireland from 1820 (when the first official records were kept) until today?

5-2 The Irish are the fourth largest immigrant group to arrive in America. What three groups surpassed them?

5-3 When the United States achieved its independence from Britain in 1776, what part of the population was Catholic?

5-4 The Irish Catholics who began to migrate to America in the early 19th century were thought of as aliens who would never fit in. Why were the Irish viewed this way?

5-5 What adjustments to life in America were the hardest for Irish-Catholic immigrants to make?

5-6 What role did Catholicism play in helping the Irish adapt to America?

5-7 From the early years of Irish immigration, Irish Americans have been among the most patriotic of America's ethnic groups. Why is this so?

5-8 Because they arrived in America already speaking English, what advantages did Irish immigrants have over other immigrants?

5-9 Irish-Catholic immigrants came to America with three great passions. What were these passions?

5-10 After their arrival in the United States, the Irish quickly acquired a reputation for a certain quality. What was this quality?

5-11 How was the Irish fighting spirit demonstrated?

5-12 What was particularly notable about the participation of Irish Americans in the Civil War?

5-13 New York State sent an entire regiment of Irishmen into the war. What was this regiment called?

5-14 What was one reason so many recently arrived Irishmen fought in the Civil War?

5-15 The name of what Irish town is used in colloquial English to describe a brawl?

5-16 What qualities were attributed to the people of Ireland years ago and help explain their political success in the countries to which they emigrated?

5-17 Until the 1960s, what distinguished Irish-Catholic families from Protestants and even from other Catholic families?

5-18 What other characteristic expressed the devotion of Irish families to the Catholic Church?

5-19 In the 1990 census, more than 51,000,000 people claimed Irish ancestry in this country. Only 12,000,000 of them were purely Irish. The remaining 39,000,000 were of mixed ancestry. What does this indicate?

5-20 By the 1970s what notable accomplishment in the field of higher education was achieved by Irish Catholics in America?

5-21 What American dialect came from the type of English spoken by the Scots and Scotch Irish in Britain?

Irish Symbols, Customs, and Legends

5-22 What color is associated with the Protestant Irish from Northern Ireland?

5-23 What color is associated with Ireland and Irish Catholics?

5-24 What symbols are associated with Irishness in contemporary culture?

5-25 What is the customary greeting among the Irish on St. Patrick's Day?

5-26 What food is it customary to eat on St. Patrick's Day?

5-27 One of the favorite Irish legends is that of the Blarney Stone. According to tradition, what happens to someone who kisses this stone?

5-28 According to legend, what did St. Patrick do when he arrived in Ireland?

5-29 What legend is associated with the leprechaun?

5-30 Two distinct classes of Irish immigrants developed in America. What were they called?

5-31 In which region of the country were Irish Americans most successful in moving up?

5-32 Why was the American frontier the area where Irish Catholics confronted the fewest obstacles in America?

5-33 In which city and region were the Irish the slowest to improve their status?

5-34 Why was it so difficult for Irish immigrants to reach their social and economic goals in this region?

5-35 How did the unfriendly attitude of people from this area affect the fate of the Irish?

5-36 Did the hostile attitude of the upper class in this region toward Irish Catholics dissipate as newer immigrant groups and southern blacks began to migrate to the region?

5-37 How did Irish-Catholic men (both the immigrants and their children) become familiar with and adjust to the established American sense of manners and behavior?

5-38 How did Irish women learn American customs and standards of behavior?

5-39 By the 1920s, Irish Americans began to mix with the mainstream of American society and lose some of their distinctive characteristics. What change in the fortunes of their Irish homeland encouraged this shift?

5-40 What factors in American society allowed people with an

Irish background to gradually fit in with society at large and gain a higher status?

5-41 What economic factors helped the Irish gain social acceptance in eastern cities where they were once scorned and despised?

5-42 By the 1930s there were clear signs of Irish fitting into the mainstream of society in eastern cities. What were some of these signs?

5-43 What were other signs of this acceptance?

5-44 The political culture and social attitudes of America run contrary to the religious culture from which Irish-Catholic immigrants came. Explain how these two cultures clashed with each other.

5-45 How have Irish Catholics reconciled their duty to Catholicism with their absorption of American cultural attitudes?

5-46 Boston College recently established a program in Irish Studies which focuses on the history and contributions of the Irish in America. What does this show about the interest of Irish Americans in their heritage?

5-47 One sign that the Irish are accepted in America is the popularity of common Irish first names among Americans of other backgrounds. Give examples of boys' and girls' first names that used to be exclusively Irish but are now common American names.

5-48 On St. Patrick's Day in many American cities, people often walk around with buttons bearing the slogan, "Kiss me, I'm Irish." What does this reflect about social acceptance of the Irish in contemporary American society?

◀ President Ronald Reagan, shown here in 1986 with Mikhail Gorbachev, the former premier of the Soviet Union, is one of 20 presidents of the United States with Irish roots. Reagan's paternal great-grandparents came to America from the village of Ballyporeen in County Tipperary.

CHAPTER

6

POLITICAL PARTICIPATION

Political Life in Ireland

6-1   Well into the 19th century, Ireland was a fragmented country. Most people lived in villages and had limited contact with other regions of the country. What social relationships are emphasized in a life of isolation, poverty, and hardship?

6-2   What was the first large political movement in Ireland? When was it organized?

6-3   Did Irish Americans have any influence on political life in Ireland?

Building the Urban Political Machine

6-4   What political phenomena closely associated with American cities and the Democratic Party were largely invented by the Irish?

6-5   How did Irish loyalty to one's family, country, and church translate into the American political scene?

6-6 What was the name of the well-known building in Manhattan where political deals were cut that directed the political life of New York City for generations?

6-7 Daniel Patrick Moynihan has compared the way Tammany Hall was run to the functioning of an Irish village in 19th-century Ireland. What were some features common to both?

6-8 In the 1850s an anti-immigrant party had some success in Massachusetts, New York state and elsewhere. What was the name of this party? To what was it reacting?

6-9 In 1894 *The Irish Conquest of Our Cities* was published in Chicago. To what does this title refer?

6-10 George Washington Plunkett, an Irish district leader from Tammany Hall in New York, once commented on how important it was to help even one family who lost its home in a fire. He added, "Who can tell how many votes one of those fires brings me?" What does this comment exemplify?

6-11 Plunkett's comment also reflects another reality of 19th-century America. What government programs to provide help to people in need existed then?

6-12 The Irish introduced a personal element into urban politics. Where did this approach to politics come from?

6-13 What problems did this approach to urban politics bring?

6-14 What are some examples of how political corruption began to influence urban life?

6-15 When were big-city political machines dominant?

6-16 During the 20th century, in order to be elected mayor of

Boston a person generally needed three qualifications. What were these?

6-17 Which mid-20th-century political figure is now considered the last and most famous of Irish big-city bosses?

6-18 Why was Daley considered a classic example of what the urban machine produced?

6-19 After Daley's death he was succeeded for two terms by politicians from the Democratic Party machine. Who won the mayor's race in 1983 and became only the second non-Irish mayor of Chicago since the 1930s?

6-20 By the mid-1980s, observers pronounced the Daley machine in Chicago dead, and Irish political control of the city a relic of past history. Were they correct?

6-21 Is there a new Daley machine today in Chicago?

National Politics and the Decline of the Political Machine

6-22 What caused the urban political machines to decline?

6-23 What other change brought about the decline of the urban political machine?

6-24 Andrew Greeley, an Irish-American sociologist and priest, commented, "Economics and the search for the good life find Irishmen filling up suburban shopping centers, not ward meetings." How does this explain the decline of the urban political machines?

6-25 Which Irish-American politician who came to prominence in the 1950s became infamous for his anti-communist witch hunts during that decade?

6-26 Joseph McCarthy was strongly backed by Irish Catholics. Why were the Irish such staunch supporters of McCarthy?

6-27 The election of John F. Kennedy as president in 1960 was a milestone for Catholics. What did it demonstrate?

6-28 When John F. Kennedy was elected president, the poet Robert Frost told him, "Be more Irish than Harvard." What did this advice mean?

6-29 In recent presidential elections, ethnic Catholics have increasingly switched loyalties. Which party do a slight majority of ethnic Catholics now support?

6-30 What seems to be the main factor behind Irish Americans switching political party loyality?

6-31 Patrick Buchanan and William Bennett are conservative activists involved in the political leadership of the Republican Party. What makes them a new breed in this party?

The Politics of Northern Ireland

6-32 From its inception, Sinn Fein has received most of its inspiration and money from what source?

6-33 The American influence on Irish politics is visible in efforts to resolve the conflict in Northern Ireland. Which Irish-American politicians have taken an interest in this conflict?

6-34 Whom did President Bill Clinton invite to America to discuss the conflict in Northern Ireland?

6-35 Ian Paisley, the firebrand leader of the Protestant Unionists in Ulster, also has an American connection. What is his link?

U.S. Presidents of Irish Descent

Did you know that 20 of America's 42 Presidents can claim Irish descent? They include:

John Adams (president from 1791–1801)
James Monroe (1816–1820)
John Quincy Adams (1825–1829)
Andrew Jackson (1829–1837)
James Knox Polk (1845–1849)
James Buchanan (1857–1861)
Andrew Johnson (1865–1869)
Ulysses S. Grant (1865–1877)
Chester Alan Arthur (1881–1885)
William McKinley (1897–1901)
William Howard Taft (1909–1913)
Woodrow Wilson (1913–1921)
Warren G. Harding (1921–1923)
Herbert Clark Hoover (1929–1933)
Harry S. Truman (1945–1953)
John F. Kennedy (1961–1963)
Richard M. Nixon (1969–1974)
Ronald Reagan (1980–1988)
William J. Clinton (1992–)

◄ Henry Ford helped found the American automobile industry in Detroit, and his manufacturing innovations, including the production line, enabled him to produce cars cheaply enough that many families could afford them. He is shown here with the first and the 10 millionth Fords produced.

CHAPTER

7

ECONOMIC LIFE

7-1 Irish immigrants to America in the 18th, 19th, and early 20th centuries usually came from which economic class?

7-2 What did the immigrants do to make a living when they arrived in America?

7-3 What two canals in the East and Midwest were built primarily by Irish workers?

7-4 What blue collar industry centered in eastern Pennsylvania attracted many Irish immigrants in the 19th century?

7-5 The late 19th century brought great technological advances to industry in the northern sections of America. It was also the age of the robber barons—capitalist entrepreneurs who amassed great fortunes building railroads, mines, and steel mills. How were workers treated during this period?

7-6 As a reaction to the exploitation of miners, a group formed and called itself the Molly Maguires. Who were they?

7-7 Where did this group get its name?

7-8 In the late 1800s American workingmen had few rights. They had to tolerate whatever wages and hours were dictated to them. It took courage, perseverance, and patience to stand up to the great industrialists and robber barons. Why were the Irish particularly suited to be labor leaders?

7-9 At the turn of the century, 50 out of 110 unions in the American Federation of Labor (AFL) were led by Irish Americans. What Irish-American man helped to found the AFL in 1886? What Irish-American woman founded the Woman's Trade Union League in the early 1900s?

7-10 What important unions have had first- and second-generation Irish Americans as their presidents during long stretches of the 20th century?

7-11 While the first generation of Irish-American men and women generally worked as manual laborers, the second generation had better-paying jobs. What changes occurred in job status from the first to the third generation?

7-12 What economic impact did the emigration of Irish people to America have on Ireland itself?

7-13 The benefits of controlling the political administration of American cities are clear if one looks at the job distribution in Chicago during 1900. What was unusual about the public labor force of the city of Chicago at that time?

7-14 Until the last generation, the majority of the police force in most major cities were descendants of Irish immigrants. Why did the Irish dominate this profession so conspicuously?

7-15 Why did police vans in the late 19th century acquire the nickname "paddy" wagons?

7-16 As the Irish moved from unskilled labor to better jobs, what professions were the most popular?

7-17 "They say, 'He's one of our own,' and they say it with pride. He's the poor Irish boy who made good and came out of the slums to wear a frock coat and sit in the governor's chair." What does this comment about Frank Skeffington in Edwin O'Connor's book *The Last Hurrah* describe?

7-18 In retrospect, what impact did political patronage have on the welfare of the urban Irish population in America?

7-19 What type of work existed for the Scotch Irish of the Appalachian Mountains?

7-20 What son of Scotch-Irish immigrants helped to launch America's first mass production industry in the Midwest?

7-21 Compared to their condition when they arrived in America as refugees from poor and famine-stricken Ireland, how have Irish Americans fared economically in the United States?

◀ One of the most popular cultural events for Irish Americans is the annual St. Patrick's Day celebration. Many cities hold parades or services, and millions of people of all ethnic backgrounds turn out each year to enjoy the festivities, as this six-year-old girl is doing.

CHAPTER

8

CULTURAL LIFE

Music

8-1 How was culture primarily passed on in Gaelic Ireland?

8-2 What form of music was very popular among the Irish as a way of remembering the folklore of ancient Ireland?

8-3 How did the circulation of ballads and poems affect Irish political life?

8-4 What experience does the following Irish folk song describe:

The Shores of Amerikay

I'm bidding farewell to the land of my youth and the home I love so well.
And the mountains so grand round my own native land, I'm bidding them all farewell.
With an aching heart I'll bid them adieu for tomorrow I'll sail far away.
O'er the raging foam for to seek a home on the shores of Amerikay.

8-5 The following lyrics come from an Irish-American folk song of the mid-1800s:

Paddy on the Railway

In Eighteen Hundred and Forty Seven
Poor Paddy was thinkin' of goin' to heaven
God bless him and if he left one child then he left eleven
All workin' on the railway, the railway.
I'm weary of the railway, poor Paddy works on the railway.

What experience does this song describe?

8-6 What event in Irish history does the following song commemorate:

Michael Collins

Oh long will old Ireland be seeking in vain
Ere we find a new leader to match the man slain
A true son of Grainne his name will long shine
O gallant Mick Collins cut off in his prime.

8-7 What Irish-American songwriter became famous in the early 20th century for his association with Broadway?

8-8 One of this songwriter's most famous songs was sung by American troops in World War I. What was the name of the song?

8-9 What sort of Irish music is one likely to hear on American radio stations in major cities today?

8-10 What is the name of the popular musical group that has performed traditional Irish folk music and ballads over the past 30 years in North America?

8-11 What was that group's most famous song, produced in 1968 and still played today?

8-12 Many Irish folk songs have become part of the American national repertoire. Name some of these.

8-13 What type of contemporary music resembles the Irish ballads brought to America by immigrants from Ireland?

8-14 What type of American folk dancing owes some of its dance steps to the Irish jig?

Writers

8-15 Which Irish American is considered America's best playwright?

8-16 Eugene O'Neill wrote many acclaimed dramas during his writing career. Name some of these.

8-17 Who was the first Irish-American writer to achieve literary fame writing about the lower-middle-class Irish of Chicago in the 1930s and '40s?

8-18 F. Scott Fitzgerald was one of the preeminent American writers of the early part of the century. What are his most acclaimed works?

8-19 Which novel by F. Scott Fitzgerald was considered autobiographical? It was the basis of a popular movie in the 1970s.

8-20 What Irish-American author wrote the acclaimed novel *The Last Hurrah?* What was the subject of this book?

8-21 Flannery O'Connor was one of many great American writers who came from the South. What made her unusual?

8-22 What is the name of the book about the childhood struggles of an Irish American growing up in the city of Limerick, Ireland, in the 1930s? It became a bestseller in the fall of 1996.

8-23 What two famous sports teams, one in professional basketball and the other a college team, have Irish names?

8-24 Sports was one of the avenues for a young man to escape the poverty and anonymity of urban life. What sport attracted many Irish-American men in the 19th century?

8-25 Who were some of the preeminent Irish-American prizefighters during the past 100 years?

8-26 By the early 1900s the Irish had become one of the dominant ethnic groups in professional baseball. What two legendary managers of Irish background faced each other in three World Series between 1905 and 1913?

8-27 Ernest Thayer wrote a poem in 1888 about a baseball team from a fictional town called Mudville and its Irish-American hero who struck out. What was the name of this poem?

8-28 What is the sport of hurling?

8-29 Because of their disproportionate concentration in America's largest cities, Irish Americans acquired a stereotypical image in popular entertainment at the beginning of the 20th century. What was this image?

8-30 Which Hollywood actor is most associated with the role of a street-smart city slicker? He played the role of George M. Cohan in one of his popular movies.

8-31 Many of the earliest comic strip characters were also of Irish background. Who was the first comic strip character created for mass circulation?

8-32 Another favorite role for Irish-American characters was the policeman, reflecting the Irish presence on police forces in most cities. What plainclothes police detective of Irish background was the central character in a comic strip? It later became a radio and television series and a movie.

8-33 What two Irish-American actors portrayed the two most famous working class characters on American television (one from Brooklyn and the other from Queens)?

8-34 *Dr. Kildare* was another popular television show (1961–1966) that portrayed an Irish-American character. Who was this character?

8-35 What movie produced in 1981, starring Robert De Niro and Robert Duvall, provided an inside look at two of the three urban institutions dominated by Irish Americans: the Catholic Church and the police department?

8-36 What men with Irish-American roots currently star in television and movies?

Intellectual Life and General Culture

8-37 What Irish-Catholic woman was considered one of this century's leading American intellectuals and gifted writers?

8-38 In the 1950s, what prominent writer and commentator founded the magazine *National Review?* He also helped create a conservative ideological movement to counter the dominant liberal ideology of the time.

8-39 Jimmy Breslin is known for what accomplishments in the world of writing and journalism?

8-40 Who was one of America's greatest architects and the founder of the Chicago School of Architecture in the late 19th century?

◀ Grace Kelly was a popular actress who starred in several films, including *To Catch A Thief* and *Rear Window.* She later gave up her acting career to marry Prince Ranier of Monaco. Grace's father, John B. Kelly, and brother, Jack Kelly, both won Olympic gold medals for rowing.

CHAPTER
9

IMPORTANT PERSONALITIES
and PEOPLE OF ACCOMPLISHMENT

Political Leaders and Public Figures

9-1 Who was the only Catholic to sign the Declaration of Independence?

9-2 In 1905 who was the first Boston-born Irish Catholic to be elected mayor of Boston?

9-3 Whom did John Fitzgerald's daughter Rose marry to start a famous American political family?

9-4 Which descendants of Joseph and Rose Kennedy have gone into American political life?

9-5 What third-generation Irishmen became presidents of the United States?

9-6 Who was the first person of Irish-Catholic background to run for president?

9-7 Which Irish-American politician carved out a long, colorful, and controversial career in Massachusetts as mayor, congressman, and governor?

9-8 The quintessential "Irish pol" and one of the most colorful speakers of the House of Representatives was an Irish American from Cambridge, Massachusetts. Who was he?

9-9 What Irish American served in four presidential administrations and is senior senator of New York State?

9-10 In 1956 President Eisenhower appointed a son of Irish immigrants to the Supreme Court. He was assumed to be a moderate on social issues, but he turned out to be one of the most liberal justices that ever sat on the high court. Who was he?

9-11 Daniel and Philip Berrigan are two brothers who are also Catholic priests. What did they become known for in the 1960s?

9-12 Since the 1960s the Irish-Catholic population has become more liberal on political and social issues. What two presidential candidates of Irish descent represented this more liberal view?

9-13 Robert Drinan was a congressman from suburban Boston and a liberal Democrat. What made him an unusual politician?

9-14 Eight American presidents were of Scotch-Irish background. Name several of them.

Entertainment and Sports

9-15 Which person of Irish background was considered one of Hollywood's greatest actors? He starred in *Captains Courageous* (1937) and *Boy's Town* (1938).

9-16 Which person of Irish background was one of the great dancers in Hollywood musicals? He starred in the movie *Singing in the Rain*.

9-17 What is the name of the Irish American who was probably the most popular singer of the 1930s and '40s?

9-18 What daughter of an Irish-American bricklayer-turned-millionaire became a movie star and married the Prince of Monaco?

9-19 What Irish pop music star, with controversial views on Catholicism, achieved international fame in the late 1980s and early 1990s?

9-20 What son of an Irish ward politician in Chicago helped establish the American League in baseball and became the first owner of the Chicago White Sox?

Military Figures

9-21 What famous frontiersmen were of Scotch-Irish background?

9-22 What great Civil War general from the Confederacy was Scotch Irish?

9-23 What son of Irish immigrants became one of the most successful Union generals in the Civil War?

9-24 What Irish-American military figure led the legendary 69th Regiment from New York State into the European front in World War I? He was also the founder of the Office of Strategic Services (OSS) during World War II, which was the precursor of the CIA.

Answers

1 ORIGINS

Ireland Under English Rule

1-1 The Celtic tribes were the first people to invade Ireland. They came around 250 B.C.

1-2 The Celtic tribes are thought to have come originally from beyond the Caspian Sea. They invaded and conquered most of Western Europe around 400-500 B.C.

1-3 The Vikings invaded Ireland in the late 8th century A.D. They helped establish Ireland's first towns, including Dublin, and its monetary system.

1-4 The British invaded Ireland in the 12th century A.D.

1-5 When the pope refused to grant the English King Henry VIII a divorce, King Henry broke away from the Church of Rome. In 1534 he established the Anglican Church as the national Church of England. He appointed himself as the leader of that church.

1-6 The religious differences between the English and the Irish only aggravated the ethnic and economic differences between the two groups. They added a religious dimension to an existing conflict over control of Ireland.

1-7 The English monarchy thought that it could more easily dominate Ireland by settling the country with Protestant loyalists.

1-8 Scottish Protestants in the north of Ireland became known as the Scotch Irish.

1-9 Other than the obvious religious differences, Irish Protestants were generally better off economically than Irish Catholics because the area where they lived was intentionally industrialized by the British. The Protestants also had a strong affinity and allegiance to the English and their political culture. The Catholics had a strong antipathy to English institutions.

1-10 Relations between Catholics and Protestants in Ireland have almost always been hostile, with periodic flare-ups of violence and public animosity. In Ulster (Northern Ireland), the Protestant majority practiced considerable economic discrimination against the Catholic minority until recently. This discrimination has declined because of official British policy and enforcement.

1-11 In the early 19th century, Irish peasants ate mostly potatoes, were malnourished, suffered from many epidemics and diseases, lived in small huts with minimal furniture, and dressed in rags.

1-12 By the mid-18th century, about 95 percent of the land in Ireland was owned by landlords, many of whom lived far away in England. Irish peasants rented land to eke out an existence by farming. Catholics were forbidden to buy land from Protestants unless they themselves became Protestants. They were forced by law to subdivide their plots among their descendants. As the Irish population grew, it had less land to support each family and became more impoverished.

1-13 The potato was Ireland's major crop.

1-14 Potatoes are good for the soil because they add nutrients to it. They feed more people per acre of cultivation than any other crop. Because they grow underground, their crop is less likely to be disrupted by civil unrest, a chronic problem in Ireland.

1-15 If a disease afflicts this one crop, peasants run the risk of starvation because there is no other crop to use as a substitute.

1-16 Gaelic was the original language of Ireland.

1-17 Irish people who became educated and those who moved to the cities or large towns generally learned English because it was a practical necessity. English-speaking merchants and landowners dominated the commercial and intellectual life of Ireland. Also, in Ireland speaking English became associated with sophistication because of its connection to the British Empire. In 1831 the newly established Irish public school system (run by the British) adopted English as its dominant language. This decision largely sealed the fate of the Gaelic language.

1-18 There have been continuous attempts to revive Gaelic since the late 19th century, largely for reasons of national pride and as a symbol of Irish identity. None of these efforts has succeeded in reviving Gaelic as a spoken or written language.

1-19 The Act of Union in 1801 made Ireland part of Great Britain and subject to the British Parliament.

1-20 The Penal Laws, passed in the late 17th century, were designed to suppress Catholic religious life, education, and political expression. Irish Catholics were not allowed to hold political office or to vote for Parliament. The Catholic Church functioned largely as an underground church during the 18th century.

1-21 Daniel O'Connell's movement obtained political equality for Irish Catholics under British rule. It succeeded in getting the Penal Laws repealed in 1829. This meant Irish Catholics were allowed to vote for representatives in the British Parliament.

1-22 After the repeal of the Penal Laws, O'Connell launched a movement for home rule. The goal of this movement was to convince the British Parliament to give Ireland complete political independence, rather than maintaining it as a part of the United Kingdom.

▼ The statue of Daniel O'Connell proudly surveys the bustling streets of Dublin, Ireland, in 1890. O'Connell (1775–1847) was an Irish political leader who in 1823 founded the Catholic Association. This group pressured the British Parliament into passing the Catholic Emancipation Act of 1829, which removed restrictions on Irish Catholics, allowing them to own property and vote for members of parliament. O'Connell later became a member of parliament, where he supported a movement to repeal the union between England and Ireland.

1-23 Sinn Fein was founded in 1905.

1-24 *Sinn fein* means "ourselves alone" in Gaelic. It refers to the desire of Irish Catholics to rule themselves without British interference.

1-25 The Protestants formed a voluntary paramilitary force called the Ulster Volunteers and threatened to fight a civil war if Ireland got full independence. They feared being left as a Protestant minority in a predominantly Catholic country.

1-26 Home rule was delayed by the British entrance into World War I.

1-27 The Irish Republican Brotherhood (IRB), later renamed the Irish Republican Army (IRA), launched a military uprising against the British as a strategy to gain independence. They didn't think they would succeed in their military campaign, but they hoped their actions would rally people behind their cause.

1-28 Most of the surviving IRB leaders, such as Pádraig Pearse and James Connolly, were executed by the British and became heroes to many Irish Catholic. Others, such as Eamon De Valera, were imprisoned.

1-29 In 1918 Sinn Fein proclaimed an independent Irish Parliament in Dublin. Meanwhile the IRA, under the leadership of Michael Collins, plunged into an undeclared guerilla war with the British constabulary force.

1-30 The six counties in the northeastern part of the island, a region known as Ulster, became a separate political entity, Northern Ireland. It was independent from the rest of Ireland and had connections to Great Britain.

▲ Gerry Adams, the leader of the Irish political party Sinn Fein, addresses a crowd of supporters in Northern Ireland in 1995. Sinn Fein (Gaelic for "ourselves alone") was founded in 1905 by Arthur Griffith, who advocated freeing Ireland from British rule. Sinn Fein played a vital role in the establishment of the Irish Free State in 1922.

The twenty-six counties in the rest of Ireland became known as the Irish Free State, an independent state with Dominion status within the British Commonwealth of Nations.

1-31 When Ireland was proclaimed a republic, it became completely independent of Great Britain.

1-32 Until 1972, Northern Ireland was a province within the United Kingdom with its own local government. The majority of the population is Protestant and supports remaining in the United Kingdom. The Catholic minority would like to be part of the Republic of Ireland created in 1949. In 1968 there was an outbreak of hostilities, terrorist acts, and general disorder in the province. The Ulster local government was suspended, and Britain took direct political control of the province. Various power-sharing ideas have been tried since then to ease tension between Protestants and Catholics.

Contemporary Ireland

1-33 Irish Protestants and Catholics continue to disagree with each other over many issues. These conflicts can be traced back to the 17th century, when English protestants were encouraged to settle in Ireland by Oliver Cromwell.

1-34 Representatives of Irish Protestants and Catholics and the British government are trying to reach a political solution to the controversy over the status of Northern Ireland (whether it should be integrated into the Irish Republic or remain part of the United Kingdom). These talks have often been halted because of terrorist acts. Both the Irish Republican Army (which supports a united Ireland) and Protestant Unionist groups (which want Northern Ireland to remain part of the United Kingdom) have been blamed for these terrorist acts. Annual parades where Protestants march through predominantly Catholic neighborhoods and celebrate historic Protestant victories over the Catholics often lead to countermarches and riots.

1-35 The British and American governments are attempting to involve Sinn Fein, the political wing of the IRA, in negotiations with some Protestant Unionists. Given that this conflict has persisted for 300 years and neither side has shown much willingness to compromise, it is hard to be optimistic about a breakthrough.

1-36 In the last decade Ireland has attracted foreign investment in hi-tech and white collar industries. This is due to its high level of English literacy, a good educational system, and a young population.

1-37 In 1995, Irish poet Seamus Heaney won the Nobel Prize for Literature.

1-38 For the first time in almost 200 years, Ireland is not exporting its young people abroad through emigration. Some emigres are returning to Ireland, and Irish people can look forward to a brighter economic future in their own country.

1-39 It has become clear to the IRA in recent years that the people of Southern Ireland have grown tired of the conflict in the North. The people in the South want the conflict to end so they can attract more foreign investment to the island and improve its image as a peaceful place. The government in Dublin is putting pressure on the IRA to come to an agreement with the Protestant Unionists.

1-40 The Irish Republic and Great Britain have generally good relations. The generation that lived under British rule has mostly died, so the people of Ireland and Britain relate to each other as political equals.

2 ARRIVAL IN AMERICA

Waves of Immigration

2-1 Irish immigrants began to arrive in Virginia and the eastern provinces of Canada in the 1600s.

2-2 Most Irish immigrants in the 18th century were Presbyterian Scotch Irish.

2-3 The Scotch Irish were looked down on by the English Anglicans (the dominant church of England), who in effect ruled Ireland.

2-4 Huge waves of immigration began in the 19th century.

2-5 From 1846–51 the worst outbreak of blight occurred in the potato crop in Ireland, and roughly one million Irish left the country, going to England and America. Another one million died of starvation or disease.

2-6 The children of non-English-speaking immigrants often learned English but not the language of their homeland. This loss of a common language made it difficult for families to keep in touch with each other for more than one or two generations after family members emigrated to America. Because English was spoken in Ireland, Irish families were able to keep close ties with each other for several generations. In addition, Irish Americans were able to read newspapers from their homeland and follow events there for generations after they emigrated because there was no language gap.

Settlement in America

2-7 Many of the Scotch Irish settled in Appalachia. Others migrated to Maryland, North Carolina, and other parts of the Southeast.

2-8 The Scotch Irish were fiercely independent, and many of them wanted to live out of reach of organized government. Their families had originally come from the Scottish lowlands.

▼ Immigrants who have passed through Ellis Island, New York, await a ferry to Manhattan and a new life. From 1846–51, about one million Irish immigrants came to the United States to escape poverty and the starvation caused by famine during these years.

2-9 Some of the settlers in the mountains lived a "hillbilly" lifestyle, living simply and frugally in old-fashioned log cabins. Others migrated farther west and became the classic frontier families of American history.

2-10 Maryland provided freedom of worship for Catholics.

2-11 The first Roman Catholic cathedral in America, the Assumption, was built in Baltimore. The cornerstone of the building was laid by John Carroll. He was the first Archbishop of America and came from the prominent Carroll family of Maryland.

2-12 In the 1850s only 15 percent of Americans lived in cities. The rest lived in small towns or rural areas. The Irish were the first ethnic group to settle predominantly in the cities.

2-13 During the potato famine, the Irish experience with agricultural life was so bad that the immigrants wanted to stay away from it in their new country. In addition, they did not have the financial resources to acquire farms.

2-14 The Irish and Germans were the two largest ethnic groups in New York City in the late 1800s.

2-15 The Italians and Jews eventually outnumbered the Irish and Germans.

2-16 Manhattan had the notorious slums of Five Points and Hell's Kitchen. Los Angeles had Boyle Heights. Chicago had Bridgeport, and in Boston, the areas of South Boston, Charleston, and Chelsea were predominantly Irish.

2-17 Very few of these neighborhoods are still Irish. Some, like those in Manhattan, have disappeared altogether through urban renewal and population change. Boyle

Heights is Hispanic. Bridgeport, in Chicago, is still heavily Irish (Mayor Richard Daley lives there), and South Boston has remained mostly Irish. However, it is the exception rather than the rule for old Irish neighborhoods to remain Irish.

2-18 The descendants of the Irish immigrants who gave the character to these neighborhoods have moved to wealthier neighborhoods in these cities or have bought homes in the suburbs.

2-19 Unlike some ethnic groups, who created upscale suburban communities, Irish Americans typically did not. Greater Boston is one of the exceptions, partly because the Irish were and are such a large part of the population of Boston. South-Southeast suburban Boston has remained heavily Irish, as have some of the wealthier neighborhoods in the city of Boston.

2-20 By the 1990s, 24 percent of the Irish-American population (and over half of the Irish Catholic population) still lived in the Northeast, the area where most Irish immigrants lived during the 19th century. However, 33 percent of Irish Americans now live in the South.

3 RELIGIOUS LIFE

▲ St. Patrick's Cathedral in New York City is the largest Roman Catholic cathedral in the United States. It was planned by James Renwick and took over 20 years to build (1858–79).

Irish Protestants and Catholics

3-1 Ireland became predominantly Christian in the 5th century A.D., when St. Patrick arrived in Ireland. Western Christianity at the time was controlled by the bishop of Rome: the Pope. As the church evolved into what is now Roman Catholicism, Ireland remained staunchly loyal to the faith.

3-2 Ireland's population grew from two million at the beginning of the 1700s to a peak of about eight million in 1830, before the potato famine. Today, 3.5 million people live in Ireland. The population has remained consistently 25 percent Protestant and 75 percent Catholic. Northern Ireland, with 1.5 million residents, is made up of 60 percent Protestants and 40 percent Catholics.

3-3 The Presbyterian Church was founded by Scotch-Irish immigrants who left Northern Ireland in the late 17th century and came to America.

3-4 The Scotch Irish who settled in the mid-Atlantic states and the South remained socially conservative and generally supported slavery before the Civil War. The New England Presbyterians were generally of Scottish stock and had more liberal views on slavery and other issues.

The Catholic Church in Ireland

3-5 Ireland has always been one of the most deeply Catholic countries in Europe. It is the only country in Western Europe where the Catholic Church has a major influence on social policy because of its strong grassroots support.

3-6 Ireland has been one of the major producers of priests and Catholic scholars in Europe in spite of its small population.

3-7   The Catholic clergy were seen as custodians of the Irish national heritage during the years of British rule. Particularly during the centuries when Catholicism was actively suppressed by the British and disparaged by the English settlers and gentry, its survival was seen by the Irish as one of their great triumphs against the more powerful British.

3-8   With the decline of the Gaelic language, Catholicism was one of two major forces (economic disadvantage being the other) responsible for molding an Irish national consciousness. Even nationalist leaders who were not devout Catholics themselves recognized its indispensable role in defining Irish identity.

Catholic Life in America

3-9   From the earliest Irish-Catholic immigration to America, the Irish have been the guardians and pillars of the Catholic Church. This is changing today because of the secularization of fourth- and fifth-generation Irish Americans and the growth of the Hispanic population.

3-10   The Irish assumed top leadership positions in the Catholic church in almost every major city in America where there was a sizable Catholic population. For example, from 1847 to 1916, every bishop in Chicago except one was Irish.

3-11   In 1900 more than 75 percent of cardinals and more than 50 percent of bishops in America were from Irish backgrounds. This was in spite of the existence of large German, Italian, and Polish Catholic populations already living in the country.

3-12   To ease resentment from other ethnic groups, Irish bishops in major cities allowed the creation of national parishes. These were churches where some elements of ethnic culture and language (other than English) were preserved. They also created territorial parishes—churches whose parishioners came from particular neighborhoods, regardless of ethnic makeup.

3-13 The church generally opposed violent Irish nationalism and instead urged support for constitutional nationalism. However, some of the American bishops supported the militants privately.

3-14 Mass used to be said in Latin throughout the world. Since the 1960s, it has been said in the vernacular (the common spoken language) of each congregation.

▼ Georgetown University is one of the many colleges and universities founded by Irish-American Catholics. The school, located in Washington, D.C., was founded in 1789 by Bishop John Carroll. The Irish were the first large population of Roman Catholics to arrive in America.

3-15 No meat was eaten on Fridays. Fish, however, was allowed.

3-16 Bishop Fulton J. Sheen broadcast his sermons over the radio and later had his own television show focusing on religious themes. He received an Emmy award in 1952 as the outstanding male personality on television.

3-17 Nationally known cardinals include: John Cardinal Spellman in New York City (cardinal from 1939–67); John Cardinal O'Connor in New York City (1984–present); Richard Cardinal Cushing in Boston (1958–1970); Bernard Cardinal Law in Boston (1985–present); John Cardinal Krol in Philadelphia (1961–1988); and Joseph Cardinal Bernardin in Chicago (1983–96).

3-18 Irish-American dominance of church leadership continued into the 1970s. People of Irish descent made up only 18 percent of American Catholics in the late 1970s, but 30 percent of the clergy and over 50 percent of the hierarchy were Irish American.

3-19 Vatican II reforms caused the church to adopt a more open and ecumenical attitude toward non-Catholics. Some traditions and rituals from the church service were abandoned, and greater congregational participation was allowed.

3-20 The reforms made by Vatican II did not have all the desired effects. While Catholics have increasingly worked with other Christians on social issues where they share concerns, attendance at mass has declined. Some regions of the country are experiencing increases in church attendance, but this is often because of growing Hispanic populations.

3-21 Along with other Catholics, not as many Irish Americans attend mass as they used to or send their children to parochial schools. Like other Americans, some of them convert to other religions or do not practice any religion. The Irish are now politically the most liberal of the ethnic Catholics and the best educated. These characteristics in America are often associated with a weakening of religious attachments.

3-22 Rules requiring celibacy and forbidding marriage for priests and nuns appear to have turned away many young people from pursuing these vocations. This is especially true among Irish Catholics, who used to be the major source of priests and nuns for the American church.

3-23 When the Irish were impoverished (both in Ireland and in America), becoming a priest or nun was a way to gain better economic and social status. Leadership positions in the church were highly respected. In the predominantly secular society of America today, religious orders don't have the social prestige they once had. Moreover, Irish Americans no longer face prejudice in business and other professions where most of them pursue careers.

3-24 St. Patrick's Day, commemorating the patron saint of Ireland, is celebrated with large parades in major American cities. The most prominent parade is in New York City, where participants march down Fifth Avenue past St. Patrick's Cathedral.

3-25 In Ireland, St. Patrick's Day is celebrated purely as a religious holiday commemorating Ireland's patron saint. In America, for several generations when the Irish were struggling for acceptance, it was an exhibition of Irish pride and defiance. Today it serves as a display of Irish ethnic consciousness, but many of the people who march in the parades are not Irish at all.

4 SOCIAL LIFE AND INSTITUTIONS

Ethnic Neighborhoods and Organizations

4-1   Parishes were church communities defined by the name of the specific church. Usually people in a specific neighborhood belonged to the local church. Since attendance at church was very high, the church became the center of social as well as religious life. Each parish supported a parochial school, if it could afford to do so, as well as its own charitable associations to help needy members of the parish. Until the 1960s, the neighborhood around the church was usually solidly Catholic and often solidly Irish.

4-2   The second most important institution for the Irish was the political machine in each city. These political organizations were closely associated with unions. Through political and union connections, the Irish were able to gain access to jobs and benefits. These jobs allowed poor Irish immigrants to work their way into the middle class.

4-3   The most common institutions in an Irish neighborhood were the Catholic church and the parochial school.

4-4   The local pub or tavern was a popular gathering place in Irish neighborhoods.

4-5   The pub provided a social gathering place for members of the working class. They shared news about events in Ireland, local political issues, and neighborhood gossip. The owner of the pub was respected in Irish neighbor-

▲ To Irish immigrants new to America, the neighborhood pub was a popular meeting place, where news and gossip about Ireland were shared and local events discussed.

hoods. He gave financial advice, made loans, and provided contacts for jobs to his clientele. He often had a role in the political machine and helped deliver votes to local politicians.

4-6 Before modern sanitation was introduced in the late 19th century, typhoid and cholera epidemics sometimes swept through urban neighborhoods. Tuberculosis and pneumonia threatened public health. Alcoholism was also a significant problem.

4-7 Irish organizations included: the Fenian Society, a number of Irish nationalist groups, the Ancient Order of Hibernians, the Knights of Columbus, the Irish Catholic Benevolent Union, and a vast network of parochial schools, hospitals, and orphanages administered by the Catholic church.

4-8 Irish nationalism was the other important force in community life for the first two generations of Irish Americans. Irish nationalist groups vied for support.

4-9 The Fenians were founded in 1858, and the Clan-na-Gael was founded in 1867. Both groups began in New York City.

4-10 The Fenians wanted to send money, arms, and men to the Irish Republican Brotherhood in Ireland, which was trying to overthrow British rule.

4-11 One group of Fenians supported the idea of a violent uprising in Ireland against the British. The other group wanted to see an invasion of Canada. They hoped this invasion would trigger an Anglo-American war in which Ireland would be liberated from British rule.

4-12 Both groups' policies led to disasters. An 1867 uprising in Ireland against the British was a failure. The small raids of Fenians into Canada were fiascos.

4-13 After these failures, American membership in the Fenians dwindled. A rival organization, Clan-na-Gael, was established. The Clan was also devoted to a violent overthrow of British rule in Ireland. However, it generally restricted itself to supporting efforts in Ireland with money and words. (This policy changed in 1916 when it supported the Easter Rising.) The Clan became influential in American Irish communities, keeping the embers of Irish national spirit alive. It survived as a social force into the 20th century and died out when the Irish Free State was created in 1922.

4-14 During much of the 19th and 20th centuries, Irish and African Americans occupied the bottom rung of the social and economic ladder in urban America. The antipathy that many Irish Americans felt for African

Americans was partly because they were competing for the same low-wage jobs. And as African Americans moved to northern cities, they often settled in poor Irish neighborhoods where rents were cheap. This meant the two groups were also competing for housing and public space.

The Catholic School System

4-15 Through its parishes, parochial schools, and social groups, the Catholic Church united people who had come from all counties and regions of Ireland into a cohesive community—something they never had been in Ireland itself.

4-16 The parochial school system was the most extensive, non-government funded, denominational school system in any modern country. It was built when most American Catholics were working class or poor. This meant that small contributions from many people built the parochial school system, rather than huge donations from a few rich people.

4-17 In the 19th century, many Irish-Catholic parents and church leaders felt that the public school curriculum reflected a Protestant outlook. Students were required to read the King James Bible, a Protestant translation. Because the teachers were mostly Protestants, Catholic parents feared their children would learn ideas that were against Catholic teachings.

4-18 About 50 percent of Catholic children attended parochial school. In some eastern and Midwestern cities, the Catholic school enrollment was greater than the public school enrollment.

4-19 Most of the faculty and staff of Catholic schools were made up of priests and nuns who lived on minimal salaries and benefits as part of their religious vows. This made it easier for schools to survive financially.

4-20 Catholics of European descent became upwardly mobile and moved to the suburbs. Some of them married non-Catholics. As these changes occurred, fewer Catholics wanted their children exposed to the intense religious

▼ A photograph of the Hatfield family, which participated in the lengthy Hatfield-McCoy feud. Both families were of Scotch-Irish descent and lived in the Appalachian areas of West Virginia and Kentucky. Hostility between the two families began during the Civil War but exploded into open violence in 1882, when Ellison Hatfield was shot while helping his brother, Johnse, to elope with Rosanna McCoy. Three McCoy brothers were captured and murdered in retaliation. After years of fighting, the communities grew tired of the feuding and lawmen began to make arrests. As more and more arrests were made, the families dropped their feud.

influence parochial schools provided. Society as a whole adopted more secular and liberal attitudes during this period, which clashed with the approach of Catholic education. Religious education in general fell into disfavor among many people of all faiths.

4-21 Many parents of school-age children feel that the public schools today do not instill discipline, respect for authority, and moral values in children. Catholic schools are famous for these characteristics, so many non-Catholic parents have been sending their children to Catholic schools.

4-22 The Irish founded the urban parochial school system as a way to reinforce their children's commitment to Catholicism in a predominantly Protestant society. Today, a large number of students from African American and Hispanic families attend urban parochial schools. Their parents are not necessarily Catholic, but they feel that the parochial schools provide a better education and moral environment for their children than the public schools.

4-23 Some of these colleges include Georgetown University, founded by John Carroll, Archbishop of Baltimore, in 1789; Fordham University, founded by the Jesuits in 1841; College of the Holy Cross in Worcester, Massachusetts, founded by the Jesuits in 1843; and Boston College, founded by the Jesuits in 1863.

The Scotch Irish

4-24 In Appalachia, clan feuds became common. These were disagreements between families, or clans, that could last for generations. Clan feuds had existed in both Ireland and Scotland for centuries, and the Scottish and Irish settlers brought this tradition with them to America. Because law enforcement officers didn't spend much time in the small Appalachian villages, clans settled disagreements themselves. Revenge was the most common response to criminal acts.

4-25 The Hatfields and McCoys kept a feud going for 30 years. Both sides carried out many acts of vengeance. Legal authorities arrested some of the offenders. The men were tried, convicted, and jailed, and the feud ended.

4-26 Most of the other Scotch-Irish descendants settled in small towns. They mixed with people of English and Scottish descent, and later with those of German descent. They produced the mainstream Protestant population that is the dominant subgroup in America today.

ANSWERS
CHAPTER

5 GROUP CHARACTERISTICS

Numbers and Descriptions

5-1 About five million immigrants came to the United States directly from Ireland. Many others came via Canada.

5-2 Only Germany, Italy, and Great Britain sent more immigrants to America than Ireland.

5-3 In 1776, America was made up of two million Protestants, 25,000 Catholics, and several thousand Jews, plus half a million black slaves who subsequently became Protestants. Catholics were about one percent of the population.

5-4 The Irish Catholics were the first large population of Catholics to come to America. American society was overwhelmingly Protestant. Catholicism was seen by Protestants as an alien and disreputable religion led by a foreign potentate (the pope). Not only that, but the Irish were largely impoverished peasants from rural counties of Ireland. They had never set foot in a city before, let alone traveled outside of Ireland.

5-5 The hardest transition for Irish immigrants to make was going from the rural environment of Ireland to the crowded urban environment of America. In rural Ireland, people were similar and knew each other through family ties and clan rivalries. In America, people came from many different cultures and lived with strangers.

5-6   In Ireland, Catholics were used to being looked down upon by the English Protestant gentry. This relationship reappeared in the eastern cities of America where people with social and economic power were primarily Anglo-Protestants who shared the English prejudice toward the Irish. By establishing the Catholic Church and its schools on a large scale, Irish immigrants created a sub-culture where they felt secure and where being Irish or Catholic was not something about which to be ashamed or embarrassed.

5-7   The Irish instinctively identified with America because it had launched a successful independence movement against the hated British. Later generations were encouraged to be patriotic by the Catholic school system. They wanted to counteract Protestant fears that Catholic loyalty to the pope would be greater than their loyalty to America. The Catholic schools also emphasized the duty of American Catholics to be anti-communist because communism was against religion.

5-8   Because they already knew English, Irish immigrants didn't have to stay in immigrant neighborhoods. They could get jobs building railroads and canals. Irish immigrants also became active in politics and union organizing much faster than other groups, in part because of their comfort with the language and the similarities between English and American political institutions.

5-9   The Irish loved their homeland, were devoted to the Catholic Church, and hated England—all with great fervor.

5-10   Irish immigrants were known for their fierce fighting spirit.

5-11   A higher proportion of Irish Americans fought in America's wars than did the rest of the population. Starting with the Mexican-American War in 1845–48, Irish immigrants and their descendants fought in American armies bravely and enthusiastically.

5-12 Irish Americans fought on both sides of the Civil War. The Union army had eight generals of Irish background, while the Confederates had five.

▼ These members of the Union Army's 69th Regiment, known as the Irish Brigade, were among the 170,000 Irish Americans who fought in the Civil War. The Union had eight generals of Irish descent, including Ulysses S. Grant and William T. Sherman, who are considered among the greatest Civil War generals; the Confederates had five Irish-American generals.

5-13 The 69th Regiment was called the "Irish Brigade" or the "Fighting 69th." Overall, 170,000 Irish-born men fought in the Civil War.

5-14 Some of the Irish soldiers hoped to gain military experience and then return to Ireland to help liberate the country from British rule.

5-15 A mass brawl is sometimes referred to as a Donnybrook.

5-16 Travelers who went to Ireland noted the "Irish wit and adaptability, a gift for oratory, a certain vivacity, and a warm human quality that made them the best of good fellows at all times."

5-17 Irish Catholics were known for their large families. Irish families before the 1960s typically had five or more children.

5-18 For generations, large Irish families often had one child who served as a priest or a nun. The family felt honored when one of its children served in the church. Positions in the church no longer carry as much prestige in the Irish community as they did in past generations.

5-19 These numbers demonstrate the extent to which the Irish population has mixed with the broader American population.

5-20 Irish Catholics had the highest average educational level of any European ethnic group other than Jewish Americans.

5-21 The southern Highland dialect heard in the Appalachian and Ozark Mountains comes from the Scotch-Irish immigrants of the 18th century. This is the dominant dialect used in country music produced in Nashville.

Irish Symbols, Customs, and Legends

5-22 Irish Protestants are associated with the color orange. This comes from their connection to William of Orange, the Dutch nobleman and English king who led the Protestant forces to victory at the Battle of the Boyne in 1690.

5-23 The color green is associated with Irish Catholics. In America, Irish people (and other Americans as well) wear green on St. Patrick's Day.

5-24 The shamrock (three-leafed clover), the Irish leprechaun (a figure from Irish mythology), and the Irish harp, a musical instrument that appears on the flag of Ireland, are all associated with Irishness.

5-25 *Erin Go Bragh* means "Ireland forever" in Gaelic.

5-26 People often eat corned beef and cabbage on St. Patrick's Day.

5-27 There is a stone at Blarney Castle in Ireland. Anyone who kisses the Blarney stone is supposed to receive the gift of eloquence and flattery.

5-28 According to legend, St. Patrick drove all the snakes from Ireland into the sea.

5-29 Leprechauns are little elves who are also shoemakers. Any person who catches a leprechaun will supposedly find a pot of gold.

Fitting In

5-30 The two distinct classes were the working class or "shanty" Irish and the middle class or "lace curtain" Irish.

5-31 The farther west one went, the greater the social and economic success of Irish immigrants and their descendants.

5-32 By the time Irish Catholics immigrated to America, a stable Protestant population had been living in eastern cities for 200 years. In contrast, the frontier was sparsely populated. People who lived there were adventurous and diverse. Life was hard, and the fixed social structure and ingrained prejudice of the East didn't exist. So Irish-Catholic settlers had broader opportunities to find their own niche on the frontier.

5-33 Irish immigrants faced the biggest obstacles in New England, and specifically in the city of Boston.

5-34 New England was the center of Anglo-Protestant social and economic power. Families and social groups could trace their ancestry back to the Mayflower. They had socially exclusive attitudes toward all immigrant groups that followed them, but they had a particular antipathy for the Irish. This was partly due to an anti-Catholic bias and also to a dislike of the cultural practices of the Irish working class.

5-35 The Irish took longer to break out of the working class in New England than in any other region of the country. They also remained in their Irish neighborhoods longer in New England.

5-36 At first, the arrival of new immigrant groups did nothing to make life easier for Irish immigrants in New England. More New Englanders were sympathetic to the plight of African Americans than to that of the Irish.

5-37 Irish men became familiar with American customs through their participation in union organizing and negotiating and through their political activity. The Irish didn't hold a majority of the electorate in any city. To guarantee victory in elections, Irish politicians had to cultivate ties to other ethnic groups. Through political ties, they became familiar with the cultures and attitudes of different American ethnic groups.

▼ The Knights of Columbus was founded in 1882 by the Rev. Michael J. McGivney. A Catholic organization, at one time its membership was primarily Irish Americans. The purpose of the Knights of Columbus is to help member families and to conduct educational, charitable, and religious activities. Today the organization has more than 1.3 million members in over 7,000 communities.

5-38 Irish immigrant women commonly worked as domestic servants. Through their work in the homes of the Protestant upper class in eastern cities, Irish women learned the manners, forms of speech, and general behavior of the dominant class in America. They shared this knowledge with their husbands and children.

5-39 In 1922 the Irish Free State was established in the southern and western 26 counties of Ireland. The majority of Irish-Catholic immigrants came from this region of Ireland. Since that region was now free from British rule, the Irish national cause became less important. Only diehard Irish nationalists were interested in the fate of Northern Ireland's Catholic minority.

5-40 The socially exclusive attitudes of American Anglo-Protestants began to soften during the 20th century. A huge influx of immigrants from southern and eastern Europe beginning in the 1880s helped change their attitudes. Anglo-Protestants began to see Irish Americans as much less frightening and outlandish than the Catholics and Jews from this new immigrant wave. The Anglo-Protestants largely bowed out of the urban political scene as well. They considered it to be corrupt, full of byzantine political alliances, and lacking gentility. The Irish were happy to be left to control the political arena.

5-41 During the Great Depression of the 1930s, many exclusive social clubs that had restricted their membership to Anglo-Protestants began to admit affluent members from other backgrounds, including the Irish. The clubs understood that without new membership, they would have to shut down.

5-42 Upwardly mobile second- and third-generation Irish were moving into better neighborhoods that were predominantly Anglo-Protestant. The old immigrant neighborhoods were increasingly occupied by newer immigrant groups or by African Americans moving to the North. The proportion of Irish Americans marrying non-Irish people began to rise sharply as well.

5-43 Many of the social clubs established in the 19th century, such as the Hibernians and the Knights of Columbus, were losing membership and in some cases dying out. The primary meeting place for Irish Americans of different generations was the Catholic Church.

5-44 Roman Catholicism is a religious culture that emphasizes obedience to a higher authority and conservative attitudes toward family life. American culture, especially in the last few generations, emphasizes individualism, experimentation, and questioning of traditional authority.

5-45 Many Irish Catholics continue to identify themselves as Catholics, but they don't follow some Catholic teachings.

5-46 The first few generations of Irish Americans were intent on becoming socially accepted by the majority population. They succeeded so well that most of their descendants have become far removed from the original culture they came from, and many are now seeking to rediscover their roots.

5-47 Common boys' names are Patrick, Sean, Brian, and Kevin. Common girls' names are Kathleen, Sheila, Eileen, and Maureen.

5-48 This saying is an indication that the Irish are now one of America's best-liked ethnic groups—in stark contrast to the 19th century when they were one of the least-liked groups. In those days, it was common in eastern cities to see signs that read, "No Irish need apply," or "No dogs and Irishmen."

6 POLITICAL PARTICIPATION

THE CEREMONY OF SUBMISSION.

▲ Tammany Hall was one of the Democratic Party's political "machines" that controlled elections in America's cities. A notorious example of political corruption, Tammany Hall controlled New York politics in the 19th and early 20th centuries. At its height in 1868, Tammany Hall controlled nearly all the public officials in New York state, and the "Tweed Ring," named for Tammany leader William M. "Boss" Tweed (depicted in this political cartoon as an enthroned tiger), stole tens of millions of dollars from state taxpayers. The influence of big-city political machines has declined significantly over the last 40 years.

Political Life in Ireland

6-1 Other than the church, clan loyalty was the dominant social force in the Irish countryside.

6-2 Daniel O'Connell founded the Catholic Association in 1823. Its goal was to use non-violent tactics to pressure the British into repealing the Penal Laws, giving Catholics the right to vote and granting home rule for Ireland.

6-3 The pragmatic and egalitarian attitudes of American society have seeped into Irish political life over the last century as a result of Irish-American influence. In addition, money has flowed to Ireland from supporters in America, particularly to the more militant factions of the Irish nationalist movement.

Building the Urban Political Machine

6-4 The Irish contributed greatly to the development of the urban political machine and the control of the party "boss."

6-5 In American urban areas, the Irish immigrants and their children were easily molded into a loyal voting bloc whose vote could be delivered by a ward boss or district leader. The urban Irish became one of the most reliable voting blocs in the Democratic Party until the 1960s.

6-6 Tammany Hall was the site where many political deals were cut.

6-7 Both Irish villages and Tammany Hall had stable, predictable social relationships where everyone had a role to play. Relationships were based on a concept of hierarchy and loyalty, where the elders were always at the top.

6-8   The Know-Nothing Party was created in reaction to an increase in immigration, particularly of Irish Catholics. It faded fairly rapidly.

6-9   This title refers to the ongoing political takeover of American cities by the Irish-run political machines. Until the late 19th century, urban politics were dominated by the Anglo-Protestant upper class.

6-10   This comment demonstrates the mixture of paternalism and cynicism that characterized the Irish approach to politics. The job of a politician was to help his constituency in whatever way possible. He didn't do this for moral reasons or out of a sense of public service. He knew it would pay off on election day.

6-11   The government didn't provide help for the needy in the 19th century. Those people who fell into poverty or became unemployed or sick relied on their extended family and charitable associations for aid. The urban political machine began to provide some of the benefits that today come from the federal government through welfare and other programs.

6-12   From their conflicts with English landlords and political rulers in Ireland, the Irish brought a hatred of aristocracy, exclusiveness, and pretensions of superiority to American politics.

6-13   The personal approach to politics also led to chronic corruption.

6-14   By the 1890s the Irish in Chicago had mastered the art of election fraud. For example, some Irish politicians owned pubs from which they urged voters on election day—with the help of drinks—to vote early and often. On occasion, dead persons were registered as voters. Cooperative policemen sometimes jailed supporters of an opponent, and as a last resort, ballots of opponents sometimes ended up in the Chicago River.

6-15 The machines flourished between 1860 and 1930.

6-16 To win, a candidate would have to be Irish, Catholic, and a Democrat. The first non-Irish mayor of Boston in this century was elected in 1993.

6-17 Richard J. Daley, the mayor of Chicago from 1955 to his death in 1976, was the most famous Irish big-city boss.

6-18 Daley came from the well-known Irish working class neighborhood of Bridgeport. He started out in politics as a precinct worker in the 11th ward and rose through many city, county, and state positions. He became mayor in 1955. Daley lived his entire life in the neighborhood of Bridgeport and never lost touch with the people who launched his political career.

6-19 Harold Washington, an African American, became mayor of Chicago in 1983. He died in office of a heart attack in 1987.

6-20 Those who predicted the end of the Daley machine in Chicago were wrong. In 1989 Richard Daley's son, Richard M. Daley Jr., won election as mayor by constructing a new coalition that reflected the changed ethnic makeup of Chicago. It included white Catholic ethnics, conservative Jews, and Hispanics.

6-21 Mayor Daley Jr. recognizes that the days of machine politics are over. He launched outreach programs to women and minorities in city hiring and contracts. But like the Irish politicians of the past, and unlike his African American opponents, he realized that the only way a politician can come to power and stay in power in an American city today is by making alliances with different constituencies and sharing the spoils of power with them.

National Politics and the Decline of the Political Machine

6-22 In the 1930s, with the inauguration of the New Deal, the federal government began to erect the modern American welfare state. This period also marked the rise of powerful labor unions with large memberships. The urban machines couldn't compete with either the national welfare state or the benefits from unionized jobs. People began to expect benefits from the government and unions as a matter of right, and didn't want to owe political machines for benefits they could get elsewhere at no cost.

6-23 Political reforms in the 20th century transferred many jobs that had been controlled by political patronage into the category of civil service positions. These jobs became subject to examinations of the candidates' merits rather than the influence of political connections.

6-24 As Irish Americans have become prosperous in business and professional life, they no longer need the economic benefits that the political machines provided for them. They are no longer as intensely involved in politics.

6-25 Joseph McCarthy, a senator from Wisconsin, was responsible for initiating this period in American political life.

6-26 The Catholic Church and school system were strong supporters of the view that communism was an evil system. However, McCarthy was eventually discredited because of his tactics, which included "blacklists" of suspected communists.

6-27 John F. Kennedy was the first Roman Catholic to become president of the United States. His election demonstrated that non-Catholics had accepted Catholics enough to vote for an Irish Catholic to lead the country.

▲ Labor leader George Meany, president of the AFL-CIO, speaks at a 1971 rally. Irish Americans founded many of the important labor unions of the 19th and 20th centuries in order to improve conditions for the working class. Because of the large number of members in each union, political bosses courted the union leadership so they would deliver votes for their candidates.

6-28 Robert Frost is understood to have meant that Kennedy should be a representative of the common man, not of the privileged classes.

6-29 While for several generations ethnic Catholics were staunchly Democratic, today a slight majority vote Republican for president. Increasingly they vote Republican at the local level as well.

6-30 As Irish Americans gained wealth and moved to the suburbs, they didn't need political connections for economic advancement or to get public services. They would rather pay lower taxes and have a smaller government. The urban Democratic Party has become increasingly dominated by blacks and Hispanics in the last 30 years.

This led many white suburbanites to switch party loyalties because they felt their interests were being ignored.

6-31 The Republican Party was traditionally dominated by older wealthy families in the Northeast, business executives, and middle-class Protestants from the American heartland. Bennett and Buchanan are urban, partly Irish, and Catholic. They are trying to expand the appeal of the Republican Party to suburban Catholics and conservatives in the North.

The Politics of Northern Ireland

6-32 Support for Sinn Fein has come mostly from Irish Americans and Canadians.

6-33 Senator Edward Kennedy, Democrat from Massachusetts; Senator George Mitchell, Democrat from Maine; Senator Daniel Moynihan, Democrat from New York; and President Bill Clinton have all been involved in attempts to resolve the conflict in Northern Ireland.

6-34 President Clinton met with Gerry Adams, the leader of Sinn Fein, the political arm of the Irish Republican Army. In Britain, Adams has been considered an accomplice to terrorism and has never been publicly invited to meet the British prime minister.

6-35 Paisley has a degree from Pioneer Theological Seminary in Illinois, which is associated with the fundamentalist branch of Protestantism in America.

ANSWERS
CHAPTER
7 ECONOMIC LIFE

7-1   Irish immigrants were mostly from the peasant class.

7-2   The men became unskilled laborers, railroad workers, canal diggers, carpenters, blacksmiths, bartenders, and railroad or factory hands. The unmarried women became servants or did factory work.

7-3   The Erie Canal and the Illinois and Michigan Canal were built primarily by Irish laborers.

7-4   Irish workers were prominent in the anthracite coal mines of Pennsylvania.

7-5   Miners, steel workers, railway builders, and other blue collar workers were often ruthlessly exploited by the owners. They were paid poorly, worked in miserable conditions that were damaging to their health, and toiled through long working days.

7-6   The Molly Maguires were a group of Irish miners who organized themselves as a terrorist organization designed to inflict revenge on the owners of mining companies and wreak havoc on the industry. They murdered foremen in the mines and disrupted mining activities until their leaders were caught. Twenty of the ringleaders were hanged, and the group was destroyed.

7-7   Molly Maguires was the name of a similar organization in Ireland that sought revenge against English landlords who were felt to be exploiting the Irish peasants.

7-8　The Irish had acquired the qualities of courage and steadfastness during 700 years under English rule. They had managed to sustain their religion and national culture in the face of great adversity.

7-9　Peter McGuire helped found the AFL with Samuel Gompers. Mary O'Sullivan founded the first women's trade union in America.

7-10　Daniel Tobin was the founding president of the Teamsters Union and served from 1907 to 1952. George Meany was head of the AFL-CIO from 1955 to 1980.

7-11　The proportion of workers in clerical, sales, administrative, and other white collar job categories rose, especially among Irish-American women.

7-12　Irish workers sent back large sums of money to their relatives in Ireland. These American dollars helped many Irish families avoid dire poverty and starvation. Money was also raised to support Irish nationalist groups fighting British rule.

7-13　Forty-three percent of watchmen, policemen, and firemen were first- and second-generation Irish, even though this group made up only 14 percent of the male labor force.

7-14　The mayors and administrators of these same cities were mostly Irish. They used the police and fire departments as sources of patronage for their supporters.

7-15　The word "paddy" is used as a nickname for an Irishman. Not only were most police officers Irish Americans, but during this period a disproportionate share of the criminals were also from poor Irish neighborhoods.

7-16 Common jobs for Irish Americans include lawyers, politicians, soldiers, policemen, and priests.

7-17 This comment describes how ethnic pride caused several generations of Irish-American voters to elect the Irish politicians who ran their corrupt and often inefficient city governments. The fictional character of Skeffington is modeled on former Boston mayor James Michael Curley.

▼ Irish immigrant laborers helped to build many of the nation's railroads in the 19th century. These workers for the Central Pacific Railroad, working from California, and the Union Pacific Railroad, working from the Missouri River, built long lines that met at Promontory Point in the Utah territory on May 10, 1869. The new tracks stretched nearly 1,000 miles and, when linked with other railroads in the East, formed the first transcontinental rail line. This photo was taken at Promontory Point. The development of railroad lines into America's West opened the frontier for settlement for the millions of immigrants pouring into the nation in the late 19th century.

7-18   The system of political patronage and cronyism that was mastered by Irish politicians made a small number of people wealthy. It helped many others avoid destitution and unemployment. In the long run, however, most Irish Americans achieved upward mobility through education and blue collar and professional careers.

7-19   The people of this region were often called hillbillies. They were quite poor. The men worked on small farms or in coal mines. They lived rather isolated from mainstream society until the 1960s, when an effort was made by the national government to pave roads, improve their education, and improve their economic status.

7-20   Henry Ford was responsible for founding the American automobile industry in Detroit at the turn of the 20th century.

7-21   Americans of Irish descent have income levels above the national average and are well represented in the professional class and the business elite. Their rise represents a complete transformation of a group that was once one of the most poor and downtrodden peoples on earth.

ANSWERS
CHAPTER
8 CULTURAL LIFE

Music

8-1 The Gaelic culture was largely an oral culture. Myths, legends, and folk wisdom were passed from one generation to the next by word of mouth.

8-2 Ballads or epic poems put to music, played in pubs and at festivals, were a major form of popular entertainment.

8-3 Ballads and poems kept both old grievances against the English and rivalries between Protestants and Catholics alive for generations.

8-4 "The Shores of Amerikay" describes the bittersweet sadness of Irish emigrés in leaving their native land to pursue what they hope will be a better life in America.

8-5 Most of America's railways were built by Irish workers.

8-6 This song mourns the death, in 1922, of Michael Collins, a leader of the Irish Republican Brotherhood, a group that fought for freedom from England during the War of Independence (1919–1921).

8-7 George M. Cohan is most remembered for his songs "Yankee Doodle Dandy" and "Give My Regards to Broadway."

8-8 The song was "Over There."

8-9 American radio stations play Irish ballads that are mainly about love.

8-10 Originally from Northern Ireland, the Irish Rovers settled in Canada in the 1960s.

8-11 The song "The Unicorn" was a poem by Shel Silverstein that the Rovers set to music and sang in their Irish brogues.

8-12 Irish-American songs include the following: "When Irish Eyes are Smiling"; "Sweet Rosie O'Grady"; "Danny Boy" or "Londonderry Air"; "Wild Irish Rose"; "I'm Looking Over a Four-Leaf Clover"; "Cockles and Mussels"; and "The Whiffenpoof Song."

8-13 Country and Western music and bluegrass music both resemble Irish ballads.

8-14 Some of the steps in American square dancing were taken from the Irish jig.

Writers

8-15 Eugene O'Neill is considered America's best playwright.

8-16 His works include: *Beyond the Horizon, Ah Wilderness!, The Iceman Cometh, Mourning Becomes Electra, A Moon for the Misbegotten,* and *Long Day's Journey into Night.*

8-17 James Farrell is associated with his best-known and tragic character, Studs Lonigan.

8-18 *This Side of Paradise, The Beautiful and the Damned, The Great Gatsby,* and *Tender is the Night* are among Fitzgerald's best works.

8-19 *The Great Gatsby* is a novel about ambition, idealism, and the influence of wealth on a person's character.

8-20 Edwin O'Connor wrote this book. It is a fictional account of the end of the political career of James Michael Curley, one of the greatest and last of the Irish urban bosses in American politics. He was elected mayor of Boston three times, a congressman twice, and governor once.

8-21 Flannery O'Connor was the only great southern writer who was Catholic. Her Catholic faith played an important part in her writing. She wrote both novels and short stories, and one of her most famous stories is *The Life You Save May Be Your Own.*

8-22 *Angela's Ashes* was written by Frank McCourt.

Sports, Film, and Television

8-23 The Boston Celtics and the Fighting Irish of Notre Dame.

8-24 Irish Americans dominated the sport of boxing until they were surpassed by African Americans in the middle of the 20th century.

8-25 In the late 1800s, John L. Sullivan fought with bare knuckles. He lost the title in the 1890s to "Gentlemen" Jim Corbett after boxing gloves were introduced into the sport. In the 1920s, Gene Tunney and Jack Dempsey were the dominant figures.

8-26 Connie Mack (Cornelius McGillicuddy), the manager of the Philadelphia Athletics, faced John McGraw of the New York Giants.

8-27 "Casey at the Bat" is the poem about baseball.

8-28 Hurling is a uniquely Irish sport that dates back to pre-Christian times. It is played with a stick and a ball and is the third most popular sport in Ireland. New York and other big cities used to have large leagues of hurling teams made up of first- and second-generation Irish Americans. Recent generations of Irish Americans no longer play the game.

▼ Hurling is an Irish sport that is played with a stick and a ball. The sport was popular in the United States during the early part of the 20th century, and many of the major cities had teams (this photo is of a 1959 game between a team from Ireland and one from New York City); however, the popularity of the sport has diminished in the U.S. over the past 30 years.

8-29 Irish characters were often portrayed as tough, street-smart urbanites.

8-30 James Cagney is the classic interpreter of this role. He grew up in one of the tough Irish neighborhoods of early 20th-century Manhattan.

8-31 The first comic strip character was Mickey Dugan from a comic entitled *Hogan's Alley*.

8-32 The comic strip *Dick Tracy* originated in 1931. Spinoffs of this strip continue to be produced in other media.

8-33 Jackie Gleason created and played the character of Ralph Kramden the bus driver, on "The Honeymooners," a regular skit within his weekly television show. *The Honeymooners* later became a television series. Carroll O'Connor played the character of Archie Bunker, the factory worker from Queens, in *All in the Family.* Both programs enjoy popularity around the world as television reruns.

8-34 Dr. Kildare was a doctor whose patients rarely died.

8-35 *True Confessions,* starring Robert De Niro and Robert Duvall, was a story about two brothers from an Irish family in Los Angeles. One became a police detective, the other an ambitious priest who fell from grace as the result of a scandal.

8-36 Irish-American men starring in television and movies include Alec Baldwin, George Clooney, Chris O'Donnell, Tom Cruise, John Cusack, Harrison Ford, Mel Gibson, Dermot Mulroney, Jason Patric, Sean Penn, Matt Damon, and John Travolta.

▲ Shows by Irish folk dancers, such as the Riverdance or the Lords of the Dance troupes, have become popular forms of entertainment in the United States and Canada in recent years.

Intellectual Life and General Culture

8-37 Mary McCarthy was part of the circle of New York intellectuals who were dominant from 1930–1960. She wrote essays, memoirs, and novels, including *Memoirs of a Catholic Girlhood* (1957) and *The Group* (1963). She is also remembered for her celebrated quarrel with writer Lillian Hellman.

8-38 William F. Buckley Jr. founded this magazine. He and most of the prominent commentators in the magazine were committed Catholics and most were of Irish background.

8-39 Jimmy Breslin is considered one of the top newspaper columnists and reporters in American journalism. He writes for the *New York Daily News.* He has also written eleven books, including *The Gang that Couldn't Shoot Straight.*

8-40 Louis Sullivan, the son of an Irish immigrant, coined the phrase "form follows function" as a philosophy of architecture. He is known for his design of skyscrapers. Frank Lloyd Wright, the renowned architect, was his student.

9 IMPORTANT PERSONALITIES and PEOPLE OF ACCOMPLISHMENT

Political Leaders and Public Figures

9-1 Charles Carroll was the only Catholic signer of the Declaration of Independence. He came from the prominent Carroll family of Maryland, which was of Irish extraction.

9-2 John "Honey Fitz" Fitzgerald.

9-3 Joseph P. Kennedy.

9-4 John F. Kennedy, Massachusetts senator and president of the United States; Robert F. Kennedy, New York senator and presidential candidate; Edward M. "Ted" Kennedy, Massachusetts senator; Joseph Kennedy, Massachusetts representative; Patrick Kennedy, Rhode Island state representative; Kathleen Kennedy Townsend, Maryland lieutenant governor.

9-5 John F. Kennedy and Ronald Reagan.

9-6 Alfred Smith ran in 1928 against Herbert Hoover and lost. His policies on certain issues weren't popular with much of the electorate, but his Catholicism was clearly a drawback as well.

9-7 James Michael Curley was the endearing, clever, and cynical political boss from Boston who was elected mayor, representative to Congress, and governor during his long career (1900–1950). His style of governing was

▲ President John F. Kennedy (right) and his younger brother, Robert, then the U.S. attorney general, review documents. In the 20th century, the Kennedy family has been the most powerful political family in the United States. Tragically, President Kennedy was assassinated in 1963, and his brother was shot and killed while campaigning for the presidency in 1968.

classic machine politics. He cajoled, threatened, paid periodic bribes, and personally intervened to secure favors for his constituents. During his last run for mayor, he campaigned from jail where he was serving time for mail fraud.

9-8 Thomas "Tip" O'Neill (1913–1994).

9-9 Daniel Patrick Moynihan is a distinguished academic, has served in four presidential administrations (Kennedy, Johnson, Ford, and Nixon), and has been elected senator for four terms.

9-10 William J. Brennan Jr. was a champion of civil liberties, the separation of church and state, and social welfare provisions.

◄ Connie Mack (left) was one of the great professional baseball managers of the early 20th century. In 1913, his Philadelphia Athletics defeated the New York Giants, coached by John McGraw (right), in the World Series.

9-11 The Berrigans helped found the Catholic Peace Fellowship in 1964. This group was one of the first to initiate protests against American involvement in the Vietnam War.

9-12 Eugene McCarthy ran for president in 1968, and George McGovern ran in 1972.

9-13 Congressman Drinan was also a Jesuit priest. His liberal views on abortion went against the official position of the Catholic Church, and he was told to leave politics or leave the church. He chose to end his formal political career in 1981.

9-14 Andrew Jackson, James Knox Polk, Andrew Johnson, James Buchanan, Benjamin Harrison, Ulysses S. Grant, William McKinley, and Woodrow Wilson were of Scotch-Irish background.

Entertainment and Sports

9-15 Spencer Tracy starred in *Boy's Town* and *Captains Courageous,* as well as many films with Katharine Hepburn.

9-16 Gene Kelly was one of the great dancers in Hollywood musicals.

9-17 Bing Crosby was the most popular singer of those years. His hits included, "Moonlight Becomes You," "Ol' Man River," "MacNamara's Band," and "White Christmas."

9-18 Grace Kelly was the actress and great beauty who married Prince Rainier. She starred in memorable films such as *To Catch a Thief* and *Dial M for Murder.*

9-19 Sinead O'Connor is the controversial pop music star.

9-20 Charles Comiskey played a leading role in promoting baseball in Chicago. One of the stadiums in Chicago is named after him.

Military Figures

9-21 Davy Crockett was the son of an immigrant from Londonderry. Kit Carson was the grandson of an Ulsterman.

9-22 Stonewall Jackson was a Civil War general for the Confederacy.

9-23 Philip H. Sheridan is considered one of the three most important Union generals, after Ulysses S. Grant and William Tecumseh Sherman. He was the top cavalry officer in the Union army.

9-24 "Wild Bill" Donovan led the 69th regiment into the European front during World War I.

Further Reading

Costigan, Giovanni. *History of Modern Ireland.* New York: Pegasus, 1969.

Fallows, Marjorie. *Irish Americans: Identity and Assimilation.* Englewood Cliffs: Prentice Hall, 1979.

Glazer, Nathan, and Daniel Patrick Moynihan. *Beyond the Melting Pot.* Cambridge: MIT Press, 1963.

Jones, Peter, and Melvin G. Holli, *Ethnic Chicago.* Grand Rapids: William B. Eerdmans Publishing Co., 1987.

McCaffrey, Lawrence J., *Textures of Irish America.* East Orange: Syracuse University Press, 1992.

McCaffrey, Lawrence J. and Thomas Hatchey, eds. *Perspectives on Irish Nationalism.* Louisville: University Press of Kentucky, 1989.

Miller, Kirby. *Emigrants and Exiles.* New York: Oxford University Press, 1985

O'Connor, Edwin. *The Last Hurrah.* Boston: Little Brown and Company, 1956.

Sowell, Thomas. *The Economics and Politics of Race.* New York: Quill, 1983.

Thernstrom, Stephan, Ann Orlov, and Oscar Handlin. *The Harvard Ethnic Encyclopedia of America.* Cambridge, Massachusetts: The Belknap Press, 1980.

Watts, J. F. *The Irish Americans.* Philadelphia: Chelsea House Publishers, 1996.

Index

Index

Picture Credits

About the Author

General Editor SANDRA STOTSKY is director of the Institute on Writing, Reading, and Civic Education at the Harvard Graduate School of Education as well as a research associate there. She served as editor of *Research in the Teaching of English,* a journal sponsored by the National Council of Teachers of English, from 1991–97.

Dr. Stotsky holds a bachelor of arts degree with distinction from the University of Michigan and a doctorate in education from the Harvard Graduate School of Education. She has taught on the elementary and high school levels and at Northeastern University, Curry College, and the Harvard Graduate School of Education. Her work in education has ranged from serving on academic advisory boards to developing elementary and secondary civics curricula as a consultant to the Polish Ministry of Education and the Romanian Institute for Educational Sciences. She has written numerous scholarly articles, curricular materials, encyclopedia entries, and reviews, and is the author of three books on education, including *Why Johnny, Jamal, and Juan Can't Read Very Well.*

General Editor REED UEDA is associate professor of history at Tufts University. He graduated summa cum laude with a bachelor of arts degree from UCLA, received master of arts degrees from both the University of Chicago and Harvard University, and received a doctorate from Harvard.

Dr. Ueda was research editor of the *Harvard Ethnic Encyclopedia of America* and has served on the board of editors for *American Quarterly, Harvard Educational Review, Journal of Interdisciplinary History,* and *University of Chicago School Review.* He is the author or coauthor of several books on ethnic studies, including *Postwar Immigrant America: A Social History, Ethnic Groups in History Textbooks,* and *Immigration.*

ELLEN SHNIDMAN has written many articles and essays on the social sciences. She graduated magna cum laude from Yale University and earned a master of science degree from the Weizmann Institute of Science in Israel. Mrs. Shnidman has written or cowritten articles on the biological sciences for a number of journals and newspapers. She lives in Rochester, New York.